Preface

The subject of young people in trouble is one that arouses much interest in politicians, the police, magistrates, teachers, social workers and the public alike. It is probably also a topic on which as many books and reports have been written as on virtually anything else. We make no apology for adding one more!

Progress in the social policy field is so often interminably slow, if not seemingly impossible. It is encouraging, therefore, that juvenile justice is an area in which major advances have been made over the past decade. Juvenile offending still remains a significant proportion of all crimes committed in the UK. Many members of the public are also extremely concerned about the fear of assault by youths on themselves or their property. However, we must maintain a sense of proportion, although this is not helped by our media, which all too frequently dramatises crime and relies on it almost as a form of public entertainment.

In contrast, as this book shows, the reality is somewhat different from the public perception: juvenile crime is decreasing; diversionary measures are successful, whereas locking-up young people (and adults) is often counter productive; and for most young people, offending is transitory and something they grow out of. These more successful ways of dealing with young people in trouble have been based on the understanding that social researchers have helped to provide.

A variety of imaginative projects now take place in the community to work with young offenders and those of their peers, who are in difficulty in other ways. These can include young people at risk of entry to local authority care, or those who have recently left care. A number of these projects are run by voluntary agencies and this book viii

is concerned with three such initiatives operated by Barnardo's in Liverpool and Chester.

This is the second publication to emerge from the collaborative research programme between the National Children's Bureau and Barnardo's. Its purposes are primarily to inform Barnardo's management and projects of how effective services are in achieving their objectives, and to help to identify ways in which they might develop. However, although these are the primary aims, the issues raised are equally relevant to a broader professional audience in local authorities, other voluntary agencies and elsewhere.

It is important to reiterate that the books in this series are very much aimed at a practitioner audience – those providing services and running them. They will, we hope, be of interest to those responsible for developing policy and other researchers. But there is too little specifically for those providing services, which enables them to reflect on their work and put their particular problems and concerns in a broader context. Janet Ames' very useful book, therefore, sets out some of the main current issues in the intermediate treatment and juvenile justice fields, which sets the context for three detailed case studies of very interesting projects in the north-west. Some highly pertinent issues are raised, which have already proved to be relevant in considering the future direction of the three projects concerned.

We, therefore, recommend this book to you and congratulate the author on a solidly researched, illuminative and well-written account.

David Berridge, Research and Development Director,
National Children's Bureau
Nora Dixon, Coordinator, Research and Development, Barnardo's.

1. Legal, politicial and practice contexts

'they keep you busy...we fill in a sheet of paper about getting into trouble, whether your mates agree with it...it is to learn about crime, not to do it...it has helped.'

'when I first came, I didn't have time to come here and go robbing...didn't have the chance.'

'it's not a palace nor nothing...it keeps you off the streets...there is always someone to talk to if you have a problem.'

Learning strategies for avoiding trouble, being kept occupied, being offered the support and interest of concerned adults; these are just three tasks for intermediate treatment identified by young people with recent experience of this multi-dimensional, social work approach.

The principal part of this book is three case studies of intermediate treatment projects run by Barnardo's in the North-West of England. The case studies consider the objectives of the service providers; describe the programmes and routines of the projects; explore the experiences of the young people attending and chart the collaboration between the Projects and other agencies. The book, therefore, is essentially a detailed examination of social work *practice* in the intermediate treatment field. It is written primarily for practitioners and policy makers in this area, rather than an academic audience, although we hope it will contain material of interest to other researchers. Material is too seldom, in our view, written specifically for those with responsibility for organising and delivering services and this, therefore, is our target audience. As we shall see later, the contents have had a significant impact within Barnardo's and the relevant local authorities in assisting with the planning and future development of these services.

In the 1970s, intermediate treatment tended to be accorded the dubious distinction of meaning all things to all people. In the 1980s, practice in intermediate treatment shifted yet again. Its focus now extends beyond methods for treating, containing, compensating or occupying young people (Downie and Ames, 1981) to include procedures for managing the juvenile justice system. Two of the centres described later contain different combinations of the old and newer styles of intermediate treatment; the third centre adopts the more recent 'justice' approach.

It is evident that changes in intermediate treatment, as elsewhere in social policy and social work practice, reflect a complex inter-lacing of existing legislation, political judgements and practice 'knowledge'.

A brief review of some main debates and developments under each of these headings is, then, the task of this initial chapter – with the aim of setting the three case study projects in some broader contexts.

Legislative backcloth

Key provisions and recommendations in government legislation, White Papers and Circulars are essential to an understanding of practice in intermediate treatment. They provide the backcloth to the different components in intermediate treatment practice; in particular:

- community-based initiatives for those at risk of entering care and/ or beginning to get into trouble with the police;
- community-based sentencing options for the courts;
- neighbourhood youth and community provision.

The Ingleby Committee (Report of the Committee on Children and Young Persons, HMSO, 1960) stressed the need for preventive work with the families of deprived and/or delinquent children, and the subsequent legislation, the Children and Young Persons Act 1963, gave local authorities in England and Wales the duty to provide advice, guidance and assistance to promote the welfare of children and to reduce the need for court appearances or reception into care. Preventive programmes with young people have proved an enduring strand of practice in what came to be known as intermediate treatment.

Intermediate treatment was first formally conceptualised in the 1968 White Paper, *Children in Trouble*, where it was described as 'intermediate between supervision in the home and committal to care' (para. 21). The subsequent legislation, the Children and Young Persons Act 1969, established these new forms of treatment by extending the scope of the supervision order. Section 12 of the 1969 Act gave juvenile courts power to include requirements in supervision orders. The supervising officer could direct a supervised person to reside for up to 90 days at a specified place and to attend at a place, or places, for up to 30 days in any year of supervision. It was the supervisor, however, who was given the discretion to decide whether and to what extent he or she exercised any powers given in the court order.

The intermediate treatment directives in the 1969 Act related exclusively to children under supervision, but the White Paper on which the Act was based envisaged that intermediate treatment would usually be provided on a voluntary basis, and an intermediate treatment requirement obtained only where the supervisor felt compulsion should be used to ensure the young person's attendance. The White Paper had suggested that 'it is probably a minority of children who grow up without ever misbehaving in ways which may be contrary to the law' and the increasing recognition of the 'normality' of a great deal of juvenile crime reinforced the need to cope with the problem within the children's environment – to prevent the progression of increasing court appearances leading ultimately to residential care. In recognition of this, it was hoped that intermediate treatment facilities would help prevent the need for children to come before the courts or to be admitted into residential care. Intermediate treatment would be a range of activities open to all children with problems and difficulties.

Notwithstanding the spirit of the White Paper, financial funding of projects was only available under the 1969 Act if the provision was for children referred from the courts. This led to local authorities in England and Wales invoking powers under previous legislation (for example Section 1 of the Children and Young Persons Act, 1963) to finance preventive projects.

Community-based sentencing options for young people in trouble were widened when, in 1982, the Criminal Justice Act introduced the Supervised Activity Order. A significant feature of this order is that a juvenile bench can specify the duration and content of the intermediate treatment programme it wishes a young offender to follow. The evident purpose of the government, in increasing the control of the bench over the content of these sentences, was to establish a broader range of credible alternatives to custody for juveniles.

The government's increased emphasis on keeping young people out of custodial institutions was evident also in the 1982 Act's directive to the courts to make custodial sentences only if the court felt:

'no other method of dealing with him is appropriate because it appears to the court that he is unable or unwilling to respond to non-custodial penalties; or because a custodial sentence is necessary for the protection of the public; or because the offence was so serious that a non-custodial sentence cannot be justified.' (Section 1(4))

The introduction of the supervised activity order was followed shortly afterwards by an injection of funds for intensive intermediate treatment. The DHSS local authority circular LAC83(3) stated that:

'Under Section 64 of the Health Services and Public Health Act 1968, the Government makes grants to voluntary bodies to support the introduction of intermediate treatment facilities that complement those provided by local authorities. New money has been made available for those grants from 1983/4 in order to help the development of more intensive IT programmes designed specifically for those young people who would otherwise go to borstal or detention centre. These resources can also help authorities to bring forward plans which are dependent upon the release of resources currently tied up elsewhere, e.g. in residential provision earmarked for redeployment.' (DHSS, 1983)

To explain a little more of the contents of the circular:

- The amount of new money made available by the DHSS was £15,000,000, to be spent over three years.
- Grants were to be made available to voluntary bodies which had obtained the sponsorship of a local authority, and would be made on the basis of £2,000 a year for each young person for whom provision was made.
- The DHSS funding for each project was to be for an initial two-year period.
- The sponsoring local authority was asked to specify its funding intentions for the schemes being set up in its area once these pump-priming grants ended. As far as the reference in the circular

to more intensive IT programmes was concerned, the projects to be funded were intended to offer more intensive community-based programmes for more serious or persistent offenders.

In 1988, the Criminal Justice Act added further limitations to custodial sentencing by the court. Thus, conditions on custodial sentencing now include the offender having a 'history of failing to respond to non-custodial penalties' and it being necessary to protect the public from 'serious harm from him'. The bench must also state in open court on which criterion the sentence is being passed. At the same time, the Act strengthened court powers for dealing with breaches of a community-based sentence. Prior to this Act, there were no penalties available to the courts for breach of an intermediate treatment requirement, other than variation or discharge of the order. Under the provisions of the 1988 Act, breaches can also be penalised by a fine of up to a £100 or an attendance centre order. The sanctions available to the court for breach of a supervised activity order requirement were also extended: the court may now pass any sentence, including detention in a Young Offenders' Institution for a period of six months. Breach proceedings have to be initiated by social services departments.

Parallel with moves to increase and enhance community-based alternatives to custody were government attempts to divert many young offenders from the court process. In 1985, the Home Office issued a circular (Home Office, 1985) to encourage increased and consistent use of cautioning. Local arrangements for implementing these guidelines are discussed later in relation to the case study projects.

For much of the 1980s then, government legislation and directives were designed to reduce the numbers of young offenders appearing in court – for example, via cautioning schemes; and the numbers sentenced to custody – for example, by creating new community-based sentencing options.

Throughout the decade, the harmful effects on young people of court proceedings and, more especially, the experience of custody were presented forcefully by a significant group among juvenile justice workers. Another element in what has been called the 'new orthodoxy' (Jones, 1984) of these practitioners was a critique of preventive programmes, such as those advocated by the authors of the 1963 Children and Young Persons Act, to meet the welfare needs of young people deemed to be 'at risk'. Preventive programmes were regarded as intrusive and potentially likely to lead to the passing of high tariff sentences on young people who subsequently appeared in court.

Government proposals for the 1990s, demonstrate an increased commitment to dealing with young adult offenders in the community. Thus the Green Paper, *Punishment, Custody and the Community* (1988) showed that, despite essential similarities in offending behaviour and the numbers involved, nearly twice as many 17-year-olds as 16-year-olds receive custodial sentences, while 16-year-olds are four times more likely to be cautioned. Proposals in the subsequent White Paper, *Crime, Justice and Protecting the Public* (1990) for raising the age limit for the juvenile court are designed to reduce the likelihood of such differential treatment. For example, flexible community-based sentencing options are suggested for 16 and 17-year-olds, whereby supervision orders *and* probation orders, with their various additional requirements, will be made available for *all* in this age group. The sentence chosen by the bench would reflect its perception of the maturity of the offender.

Finally, 'prevention' remains a key element in official plans for combatting offending. Thus the Children Act 1989, passed onto the statute books as this research programme was nearing completion, stipulates

'...Every local authority shall take reasonable steps designed:
(a)   to reduce the need to bring –
     (i)   proceedings for care or supervision orders with respect to children within their area;
     (ii)   criminal proceedings against such children;
     (iii)   any family or other proceedings with respect to such children which might lead to them being placed in the authority's care; or
     (iv)   proceedings under the inherent jurisdiction of the High Court with respect to children;
(b)   to encourage children within their area not to commit criminal offences; and
(c)   to avoid the need for children within their area to be placed in secure accomodation. (Schedule 2)

How local authorities will interpret and implement these provisions remains to be seen. The legislation does, however, appear to justify care-related and youth and community work initiatives. These have persisted in the practice of intermediate treatment and, notwithstanding the arguments of the 'justice' lobby, appear to be often implemented in tandem with elements of the 'justice' approach.

Trends and debates in social policy

The detail of debates in juvenile justice will emerge from, and be discussed alongside, the three case studies in Chapters 5, 6 and 7. Mentioned here are two key features of welfare policy and provision in the 1980s and early 1990s which have shaped all welfare developments.

First, the Conservative Government adopted economic policies which emphasised the importance of the free market and implemented related social policies – 'rolling back' the welfare state. The notion of the free market is based on the idea of consumer sovereignty operating through the mechanism of supply and demand. In a free market there should be no interference by the state or other monopoly interest. What is required is a minimum state that will safeguard the market by guaranteeing law and order and by framing laws that will facilitate the functioning of the market. The private sector is viewed as wealth creating – in contrast, the welfare state is regarded as both unproductive and reliant on income raised from the productive sector. In short, the welfare state hinders the operation of a free market. Further, a monopoly of welfare services is thought to foster inefficiency.

The policy solution preferred by the Conservative Party has been to reduce state interference in welfare services and to encourage strong family ties, so that families would take increasing responsibility for the welfare and behaviour of their members. Support for the voluntary sector is part of the logic of this ideological approach and derives from the values of encouraging the morality of individual initiative, rather than dependency on the welfare state.

The general trend of public expenditure after the Conservatives came to power in 1979 accorded with these policies. Education, housing, transport and social services experienced 'real' cuts, while the institutions of defence and law and order had 'real' increases in expenditure. Substantial grants were made to voluntary agencies to further particular government objectives. A clear example, linked to the law and order initiatives, was the monies provided via the DHSS LAC(83) initiative already described (see Pitts, 1988, p 55). It was consistent also that strategies for private funding – payroll giving to charity is one example – were encouraged.

In broad-brush terms, the policy backcloth to the case studies described in this book was of tightened expenditure on personal social services; an emphasis on law and order; increased stress on family responsibility and a welcoming of voluntary sector initiatives and interventions, especially where these advanced government objectives.

The second issue was the long-term shift in policy away from the care of vulnerable groups in institutions, and towards their care in the community. This shift could be seen as meeting two, rather disparate, objectives. As far as young people are concerned, it helped to resolve professional and humanitarian concerns that discretionary social work decision-making may have led to young people spending unnecessary and increasing periods of time away from home, with adverse consequences for them. (Thorpe et al, 1980). Simultaneously, it held the promise of proving a cheaper option for a government concerned with cutting public expenditure – even though many commentators have argued that *good quality* community care is *not*, necessarily, cheaper.

The feasibility of care in the community was proved throughout the 1970s and 1980s, when groups previously cared for in institutional settings were placed in the community. To focus on children in the care of the local authority – in 1977, children living in community homes in England represented 33 per cent of the total in care, compared with 34 per cent fostered with non-relatives. By 1987, the proportion in community homes had fallen to one fifth (20 per cent) and the proportion fostered with non-relatives had risen to 53 per cent. (Department of Health, 1987) This relative increase in fostering encompassed a broad range of children, including difficult and delinquent teenagers fostered under special schemes.

These two social policy trends are highly relevant to an understanding of the case studies reported here. The centres described were all established under the aegis of a major voluntary organisation – Barnardo's – with two of them receiving grant aid under the LAC(83) initiative. Furthermore, each of the centres aimed to provide care in the community for adolescents who might otherwise be removed from their homes.

A range of practice

A national survey of intermediate treatment, undertaken in the mid-1980s by a Cambridge University research team, clearly demonstrated a wide range of practice in intermediate treatment. A five-fold typology of practice was derived from the study findings:

'I   *Prevention Pure* Predominantly needs based, with a welfare-treatment ethos. Little interest in clients' status *vis-à-vis* the juvenile justice system. No emphasis on systems intervention or awareness of possible undesirable outcomes from welfare-based intervention. No serious attempt to compete with custody/residential care.

II   *Prevention Plus* Still needs-based and with a welfare-treatment ethos. Significantly more interest than 'prevention pure' in juvenile justice system links and/or in a certain view of alternatives to custody and care; but such developments are nevertheless perceived within a predominantly welfarist ethos (as in the Personal Social Services Council (1977) report).

III   *Alternatives to Custody and Care Pure (AtCC Pure)* IT seen as exclusively for those at serious risk of custody/residential care. In most areas, IT perceived as offenders only, but in a few, also for non-offenders at serious risk of s.1(2) care orders. Programmes tend to be offence-focussed, not need-focussed. To prevent stigmatisation and punitive disposals, the notion of the 'least restrictive alternative' is often advocated, and this leads to the use of systems approaches, the development of diversion from court, etc. Preventive work with non-offenders may be undertaken by such authorities... but if so will never be called IT, and may not be called prevention.

IV   *Alternative to Custody and Care Plus (AtCC Plus)* Has many similarities with category III above, especially in the primary emphasis on IT as an alternative to custody or care. But IT is also seen as appropriate for a 'medium-range' of offenders appearing before the juvenile court (and, occasionally, also for non-offenders appearing before the juvenile court in care proceedings). 'Preventive' work, again, is not allowed as part of the IT programme.

V   *Broad-based* This category comprises at least the following two key elements:
i) a recognition of the importance of targeted IT provision aimed at being an alternative to custody or care; but such provision is seen as independently important, and not simply subsumed within a preventive philosophy as in the 'prevention plus' category;

ii) a retention also of preventive work with non-offenders, the 'at risk' etc., as a part of the intermediate treatment remit. The combination of these two elements makes the broad-based category distinctively different from both preventive and AtCC policies.' (Bottoms, 1990, p.11)

Bottoms and his research team suggested that just over half of all social services departments surveyed offered 'AtCC Pure' *or* 'AtCC Plus' provision, but that the largest single category was 'broad-based'.

The Cambridge findings alert us, then, to the considerable variety of activities being undertaken in the name of intermediate treatment during the 1980s. Two of the key questions in this book are:

• Why was there such a range of practice activity?
• What were the goals which practitioners hoped to achieve?

The study and its findings

The task of the research study was to review intermediate treatment provision in three centres in the North-West of England – two in Liverpool and one in Chester. First of all, some information is presented to indicate where the small sample of young people attending these centres fitted into the national picture (*see* Chapter 2). The research approach adopted in the study is then explained (*see* Chapter 3).

The three centres, funded jointly by Barnardo's and the relevant local authority, were established at different times during the 1980s. Their locations, starting dates and objectives are summarised in Table 1.1.

The table clearly shows that the centres were united in their primary objective, of working to keep young offenders out of care and custody by offering credible community alternatives. Centres differed in their secondary objectives – one worked solely with young offenders, the other two worked both with offenders and other young people who were experiencing particular difficulties in their personal lives. This variation in objectives reflected a combination of historic and contemporary factors including, central and local government policies, social services district management objectives and Barnardo's own priorities. A literature review of policy, practice

Table 1.1 The centres and their objectives

	North City	Boughton Hall	Speke
Location	North Liverpool	Chester	South Liverpool
Year opened	1986	1983	1980
Primary aim	To provide credible community alternatives to care and custody for young offenders aged 10–17 years.	To reduce the numbers of children who receive custodial sentences or who are made subject to care orders as a result of their delinquency	To reduce the number of juvenile offenders aged 10–17 years who are committed to care and custody.
Secondary aim	To ensure monitoring of the juvenile justice system: to check areas of need, the effects of intervention and possible ways of influencing local practice.	To reduce the numbers of children of secondary school age who are removed from home for reasons other that their criminality.	To work with any young person referred to the centre, who is experiencing difficulties with life and the problems of adolescence.

and research materials helps set these historical and contemporary debates in context (see Chapter 4).

A detailed account of the objectives of each centre, how these emerged, and how they were interpreted and implemented, follows and is the main task of this book (*see* Chapters 5, 6 and 7).

Following the detailed, descriptive accounts of each centre's work, similarities and diversities in the centres' policies and practice are highlighted in order to raise some key issues of debate (see Chapter 8).

In conclusion, Chapter 9 focuses upon the significant findings and implications of the case studies.

2. The national scene

This chapter presents some national data to help establish whether the small sample of young people attending the case study centres can be regarded as broadly reflecting patterns of attendance at intermediate treatment (or juvenile justice) centres nationally.

The young people attending the three intermediate treatment centres in this study divided, broadly, into:

- the juvenile justice population: that is, known offenders;
- the welfare population: that is, young people with relatively severe care-related problems;
- the youth and community population: that is, local youngsters, and other young people known to the social services departments, whose problems were generally deemed less urgent.

As far as the juvenile justice population was concerned, attendance at one of the case study centres generally represented one step on a ladder of penalties for offending. Some national data are presented to illustrate recent patterns of offending and sentencing procedures and to give an indication of what proportion of young offenders are dealt with in the community. In the next two sections, the whole population of young people attending intermediate treatment centres across the country is described briefly, using recently published findings from a survey conducted by Cambridge University. (Bottoms and others, 1990)

One last introductory point – the three case study centres have been, and will be, collectively referred to as intermediate treatment projects or centres, the title they were given by Barnardo's. The staff at North City, however, felt their work was more accurately described in terms of juvenile justice rather than as intermediate treatment. In summary, this was because they dealt exclusively with known offenders. They did not undertake any preventive or youth work programmes which – as we have seen – have historically formed part of intermediate treatment. For this reason, the North City Project will sometimes be referred to specifically as a juvenile justice project or centre.

The juvenile justice population

The primary objective of all three centres in the study was to offer alternatives to custody for juvenile offenders. A significant proportion of the young people included in the study had, therefore, come to the attention of the police because of their offending. They were attending the centres *either* as part of an agreed package to divert them from the courts, *or* to fulfil a sentence of the court. Where do these particular groups of young people fit into the total population of juvenile offenders?

The numbers of juveniles admitting, or found guilty of, offending dropped by over a third during the decade between 1978 and 1988. In 1978 143,500 males aged 10 and under 17 were found guilty of, or cautioned for, indictable offences. By 1988 that number had dropped to 99,200 young males. The equivalent figures for young females were, in 1978, 33,600 and, in 1988, 20,100. The greater part of this drop in numbers occurred in the four years between 1984 and 1988. The total of 169,200 males and females in 1984 had decreased by 1988 to 119,300 (Criminal Statistics, England and Wales, 1988).

This drop can be accounted for, in part, by a reduction in numbers in the relevant age group. It is also the case, however, that crime rates, which take into account the demographic changes, have fallen. In 1988, around 28 in every 1000 young persons aged 10–16 were known to have committed an indictable offence – the comparable figure in 1978 was 32 per 1,000 young persons (*see*, for example, NACRO, 1989a).

The profile of indictable offences committed by these young male and female offenders show that the offences were often *relatively* minor. Thus, theft and handling of stolen goods dominate. In 1988, such offences accounted for nearly two-thirds of those committed by males (66 per cent for those aged 10–13 inclusive, and 58 per cent for those aged 14 and under 17 inclusive) and for four-fifths of those committed by females (85 per cent for those aged 10–13 and 76 per cent for those aged 14 and under 17). The second most frequent offence perpetrated by males was burglary, which accounted for nearly a fifth of offences (19 per cent) in both the age-groups referred to above. The pattern of offending for young women shows violence against the person to be slightly more frequent than burglary. Violence against the person accounted for 6 per cent and 12 per cent of offences of the 10–13, and 14 and under 17 age-groups respectively. Burglary amounted to 5 per cent of the offences of both these age-groups.

It was noted in Chapter 1 that, during the 1980s, various measures were introduced to enable troubled and delinquent adolescents to be dealt with in the community. As regards the implementation of such measures, the national picture is quite complex.

First, it is clear that there has been a substantial increase in the cautioning of young people for offences. By 1988, the cautioning rate for all males under 17 years was 66 per cent; the corresponding figure for females was 84 per cent. These figures refer to the percentage who were cautioned of all those who were found guilty by the courts *plus* those who, having admitted their guilt, were cautioned. The overall trend towards increased cautioning remains true despite a reduction of 3 per cent in the cautioning rate of girls between 1987 and 1988, and considerable regional variation in cautioning practice (NACRO, 1989a).

Table 2.1 summarises trends in community-based sentencing between 1978 and 1988, for males aged 14 and under 17 who were convicted for indictable offences. The figures show a proportional increase in the use of absolute and conditional discharges, and in the making of attendance centre orders. There has been a proportional decrease in the use of fines. Community Service Orders have been available as a disposal to the juvenile courts for older adolescents since 1983 and there has, proportionally, been a gradual increase in their use since that time. The percentage of supervision orders made has increased also.

The general trends in the sentencing of females are similar, with the exception that there has been a relative decline in the use of supervision orders for females aged 14 and under 17 years – from 22 per cent in 1978, to 18 per cent in 1988. Another important difference is that there are far fewer, adolescent females appearing in court. In 1988, 29.6 thousand males aged 14 and under 17 years were sentenced for indictable offences in England and Wales, as compared with 2.9 females of the same ages.

Table 2.1 Community-based sentences passed on males aged 14 and under 17 years in England and Wales, as a proportion of all sentences passed

Sentence passed	1978 %	1988 %
Absolute or conditional discharge	19	25
Supervision order	14	18
Fine	39	22
Community service order	_*	5
Attendance centre order	11	16

*Community Service Orders have been available to the courts as a disposal for older adolescents since 1983 only.

Source: Criminal Statistics for England and Wales, 1988.

In considering all community-based options, it is worth returning to the increasing number of offenders who are being dealt with via cautioning schemes. This phenomenon is apparently not simply a consequence of 'net-widening', that is drawing to official attention those young people who might otherwise have been dealt with informally (see, for example, Bottoms and others, 1990). It is important, then, to remember this increase in the use of cautioning when evaluating the comparatively small increase, during most of the 1980s, in the proportional use of community-based sentences – Table 2.1 indicates an increase of around 3 per cent in the passing of such sentences on males aged 14 and under 17 between 1978 and 1988. For, if the use of cautioning and community-based sentencing are taken together, it is evident that there is a greater proportional use of options for dealing with young offenders in their communities.

Finally, the figures on sentences passed on males aged 14 and under 17 given in Table 2.2 show that – despite the introduction of new community-based sentences, and despite a dramatic drop in the number of young males receiving custodial sentences – the rate of custodial sentences, as a proportion of all court sentences for this group, has remained almost stable. Similarly, though the numbers are small – at most 100 each year, the rate of custodial sentences passed on females aged 14 and under 17 has slightly increased. The overall drop in numbers sentenced to custody is explained, largely, by the drop in numbers appearing in court (itself a significant change) and, to a lesser extent, by the drop in numbers in the relevant age group. (Richardson, 1989)

In some contradistinction to this general trend, the rate of custody has dropped in areas where LAC(83) initiatives were implemented. NACRO's Juvenile Crime Section have reported that between 1982 and 1987, there was a significant fall – of around 50 per cent – in the use of custodial and care order disposals in Initiative areas. (NACRO, 1989b) Certainly, the North City Project, funded under this Initiative, achieved a nil custody rate in its area in 1989.

Table 2.2 Custodial Sentences passed on young persons, aged 14 and under 17, being sentenced for indictable offences in England and Wales

	1979 Numbers (thousands)	%	1988 Numbers (thousands)	%
Males	6.9	12	3.2	11
Females	0.1	1	0.1	2

Source: Criminal Statistics for England and Wales, 1988

How typical was the sample of young people in the case studies? The juvenile justice populations at the three centres were predominantly male and White. As has already been noted, the gender bias is typical of the total population of young offenders.

The extent of the racial skew in the case studies is harder to estimate. NACRO has shown that Black young people are over-represented in all aspects of the juvenile justice process. It is noted that they receive custodial sentences for less serious offences, and with fewer previous convictions, than White youths. NACRO has pointed out also that only five per cent of places on LAC(83) project programmes (15 out of 302) were filled by Black juveniles. (NACRO, 1987(b) and *see* Pitts, 1990). Locally, in Liverpool, of 91 young people whose cases were considered by the juvenile liaison or cautioning panels in 1989, four were Black and 87 were White. The belief of the North City Project leader, based on preliminary evidence which she has collated, was that Black juveniles in

Liverpool may move through the juvenile justice system to prosecution more rapidly than White juveniles. (Rivers, personal communications, 1990). This conclusion, albeit based on limited evidence, is clearly disturbing and deserves further investigation.

The care-related and youth and community populations

The second group of young people attending two of the three case study centres consisted of those attending on care-related grounds – that is, their attendance was designed for one of three reasons:

- to alleviate serious domestic difficulties and prevent their entering local authority care;
- to offer additional support while they were in the care of the local authority;
- to help them at the point of their leaving care.

The third group was, again, represented at just two of the three centres. This was the group of young people who simply attended youth club, summer holiday or other activity programmes. They might have come to the notice of a welfare agency or, particularly in Speke, happened to live in the neighbourhood of the project. In general terms their involvement was designed to alleviate family stress, by offering them some congenial pursuits and, hence, reducing opportunities for getting into trouble.

As we will see in later chapters, the presence of young people at the intermediate treatment centres for reasons other than their criminality was generally at the behest, or with the knowledge, of district social services staff. In general, these young people attended on a voluntary, rather than statutory basis – though the families of young people on the fringes of care might have felt there was some official pressure for their children to attend.

National data from official sources is patchy about the numbers of young people attending intermediate treatment centres for care-related reasons or for youth work programmes. The most recent and comprehensive information about the total intermediate treatment population in England and Wales comes from the Cambridge survey which was undertaken in 1984/5. (Bottoms and others, 1990). Some of the findings from the survey help establish how the young people and programmes at the case study projects relate to a national profile of intermediate treatment.

Some findings from the Cambridge survey

The findings reported here are mainly about what Bottoms and colleagues called the smallest 'units of provision' in intermediate treatment. If an intermediate centre was running three separate groups on different days, presumably with different objectives, for the purposes of the Cambridge survey each group was defined as a 'unit of provision'.

The research team obtained information about 1,218 units of provision and 8,395 young people attending those units. These results offer, the survey authors judge, 'extensive national coverage'. Most of the provision surveyed was social services led (82 per cent) but probation and voluntary sector facilities were also covered.

The Cambridge findings are detailed and complex. However, three issues from the range of material analysed by the researchers are of particular interest in evaluating the results of our case studies:

- What were found to be the main tasks and aims of intermediate treatment?
- What programmes were organised to meet these objectives?
- What were the characteristics of young people attending these programmes?

Tasks

The Cambridge results break down the nature or tasks of the units of provision. The pre-coded responses, to which multiple answers were allowed, were as given in Table 2.3. These responses suggest a wide range of tasks and objectives in intermediate treatment.

Other findings from the survey show that only a third of the units of provision had, what might be termed, specialised functions. Thus, 13 per cent were coded as 'heavy end' only; 11 per cent as 'preventive' only; and, 9 per cent as 'medium range' only. (Bottoms, 1990, Table 23)

It follows that a significant proportion of units of provision were catering for mixed client groups. It was estimated that just under a half of the units of provision, 46 per cent offered services to a mix of offenders and non-offenders.

Aims

What were the aims which project leaders had in their work with young people? In response to an open-ended question, the Cambridge researchers found that the most important aims were:

- 'improving personal functioning' – the single most important aim, mentioned by 47 per cent of the respondendent;
- reducing criminal behaviour/changing attitudes to offending (30 per cent);
- improving social and practical skills (25 per cent);
- developing constructive use of leisure (25 per cent);
- acting as an alternative to care and custody (21 per cent).

Table 2.3 The Cambridge survey findings on tasks in intermediate treatment

	%
Diversion from court (for example, caution and voluntary IT; pre-court reparation and so on)	23
Preventive (for example, IT with children at risk of delinquency, truancy and so on, work with unemployed youth)	48
Medium range (for example, supervision order with IT, whether or not as a court requirement, but IT not seen as a direct alternative to custody or care)	50
Heavy end (for example, IT as a direct alternative to custody or care)	40
Detached community project	5
IT for assessment	12
IT as after-care or as follow-up to previous IT	18
Other	11

Source: adapted from Table 24, Bottoms 1990.

The authors note that the emphasis on personal functioning was said to be of importance even in work with the 'heavy end'. They conclude that, although the 'new orthodoxy', prominent at the time of the survey, focused on ending unwarranted intervention in young people's lives:

'...when young people are actually received in IT programmes, it is not surprising project workers will aim to improve their personal functioning in a high proportion of cases.' (Bottoms et al, 1990, p 43)

This comment anticipates a finding in the LAC(83) project described here, the North City Project.

The content of programmes

The four most significant components of the programmes were said to be:

- discussion (mentioned by 44 per cent of project leaders);
- practical or creative activities (mentioned by 38 per cent),
- social skills education (mentioned by 35 per cent);
- individual work (mentioned by 33 per cent).

Focusing on offending behaviour was reported by 15 per cent, though it should be remembered that not all units were working with known offenders. Motor vehicle project work was referred to by 6 per cent. Less than one per cent of units of provision were said to be involved in reparation.

The young people

More than three-quarters (6,392, 77 per cent) of those attending the projects surveyed were male; and just under three-quarters (5,881, 71 per cent) were aged 14 to 16 years. Table 2.4 displays the reasons given for young people's initial contacts with projects.

The reasons for attendance were rather different between young men and young women in the sample. More than half (55 per cent) of male attenders were the subject of supervision orders, with or without requirements, as compared with less than a fifth (18 per cent) of female attenders. Around a quarter of males (24 per cent) but well over half (60 per cent) of females were said to be attending voluntarily.

Table 2.4 Cambridge survey findings on reasons for contact

	%
On a supervision order with an intermediate treatment or supervised activity requirement.	30
On supervision orders with no additional requirement.	16
Other link with the juvenile justice system; such as being the subject of a caution or a deferred sentence.	17
Attending voluntarily.	32
Attending for 'other' reasons	5

Source: adapted from Table 41: Bottoms 1990.

   No information about ethnic groups was collected in the
Cambridge survey.

Conclusion

The information reported here is a very small part of the wealth of
data analysed by the Cambridge team. The variety of approaches
reported in the Cambridge survey ensure that the case study findings
will not be seen as atypical. Moreover, there are some dominant
trends in the survey findings which, as we shall see, are replicated in
our case studies. Significantly, these include the range of objectives
and client groups and a predominance of male participants.

3. Research methods

Barnardo's commissioned the National Children's Bureau to 'examine work processes and outcomes' in their three intermediate treatment centres in the North-West of England. As the research brief clearly stated, the resulting research should directly inform policy and practice. The sponsors were seeking

'...material which will assist the North-West Division to consider the different approaches of the Speke, Boughton Hall and North City IT Projects, when it is considering developmental and resource allocation issues.

To use the material for practice and policy development purposes.

To consider the role of the voluntary organisations when providing intermediate treatment services.' (Dixon, 1988)

This chapter discusses what data collection methods were employed to provide relevant data and, also, some methodological problems encountered in fulfilling the research objectives.

During the course of the research, methodological problems and issues of policy and practice were debated at the regular meetings of the small research 'advisory' group, which comprised management and fieldwork staff from Barnardo's North-West Division, and representatives from Barnardo's head office research and development staff. As each case study was completed, the findings were also shared with social services staff from the relevant local authorities. The reports on each centre, thus, provided the focus for discussions between the local authorities and the voluntary agency about the future direction of the three projects.

Examining work processes

The investigation of work processes at the three centres demanded patient work on the part of the researcher and, equally, on the part of the subjects of the research – especially the project staff and young people attending the centres. This aspect of the data collection raised some issues of access and confidentiality, but no particular methodological challenges.

At each of the case study projects, the researcher familiarised herself with the range of work undertaken by staff with young people. She also explored the different perspectives on the work of the projects held by the staff, by the young people attending the project and by representatives of key agencies with whom the project staff worked.

The research stance in each of the three projects was akin to ethnographic studies in social research – observing the subjects of study and collecting a variety of information in order to build up as full a picture as possible of the objectives of the projects, their resources and their methods of work. (*See,* for example, Bresner; Buchanan, Boddy and McCalman; and Turner; in Bryman (ed.), 1988.)

The research materials collected and analysed included fieldwork notes on discussions the researcher had:

- with the project staff;
- with young people attending the projects' main programmes;
- with the projects' volunteers;
- with representatives of the local social services district staff;
- with the police;
- with education's social work services;
- with magistrates who had close associations with two of the centres.

At each of the projects, the researcher had access to:

- documents describing the work, past and present, of the centres;
- recorded information about the young people attending;
- monitoring information on the juvenile justice systems in the two cities;
- other statistical data about the socio-economic characteristics of the social services districts served by the projects.

These materials were supplemented by the researcher's recorded observations of work sessions with young people, of juvenile and cautioning panel meetings and of daily activities in the projects.

Of the three centres, the Speke and Boughton Hall projects proved more complex to research than the North City Centre. One reason for this was that the latter centre focused solely on working with young people who had come to the notice of the police, while the other two centres offered a variety of programmes for different groups of young people. It was also the case that Speke was the first of the projects to be studied and the researcher was, in effect, piloting her research approach. As is explained below, various important lessons were learned during this research phase about the feasible scope of the study. By the third stage of the fieldwork, at Boughton Hall, the research methods for examining the work at the project were well-established. Gathering information about collaboration between the Project and the local social services department was initially complicated a little, however, by changes in personnel and joint working procedures following a re-structuring within the social services department.

The task of investigating the work of the three centres, for example obtaining the trust and cooperation of the young people, was not always straightforward. The study objectives remained constant but the researcher refined her research strategies slightly as the research progressed. Thus, at North City and at Boughton Hall, the researcher concentrated on talking with young people during their normal sessions at the projects. Discussions with some other family members took place, as at Boughton Hall, when they were themselves participating in a programme run by the project. The researcher did not attempt to undertake, outside the project, the interviews with young people and their families envisaged in the initial research design, but which she had found difficult to organise within a restricted research timetable in Speke. The prime responsibility of the projects was the young people who were their main customers – consequently, the process of providing services for them was the researcher's prime concern too.

In all three centres the fieldwork, whatever its inevitable limitations, yielded a considerable quantity of information. By no means is all that information used in the descriptions of the projects given in the following chapters. The accounts given, however, attempt to be faithful to the implications of all the information collected.

Evaluating outcomes

The second task in the research brief was to attempt to examine outcomes. The researcher foresaw, at the outset of the study, significant problems in attempting to obtain and interpret standard measures of outcome – such as re-offending rates or behavioural change. This section describes, first, some of the acknowledged difficulties associated with measuring outcomes of intermediate treatment and how these problems were confirmed during the fieldwork; and, secondly, how these challenges were met.

Evaluating the outcomes of any social experiment is problematic. The conclusions drawn tend to be tentative and even contradictory. Rutter and Giller's major review of research materials on juvenile delinquency, for example, was unable to identify clear evidence of the relative effectiveness of custodial, residential and community-based treatment or care programmes

'A wide range of corrective, punitive, therapautic, and supervisory interventions are being employed with young offenders, but in most cases information is lacking on whether one approach is better than another.' (Rutter and Giller, 1983, p.354)

Why is it so hard to monitor and evaluate the success of such programmes and, in particular, intermediate treatment programmes? A prerequisite of successful evaluation would seem to be agreement about the objectives participants wish to achieve. The experience of the case studies, and a reading of the relevant literature, suggest a lack of agreement over the objectives of intermediate treatment. While the general public, the police and the courts of law arguably perceive an important objective of intermediate treatment to be to work with young people to reduce levels of offending, not all practitioners are in accordance with that precise objective. For example, keeping young people out of custody has been thought by a significant group of juvenile justice workers to be more important than the work which is undertaken with young people during project programmes. For, it is reasoned, most young people simply 'grow out' of offending.

The objective of reducing levels of delinquency is not, then, universal. It will, nevertheless, serve to illustrate yet further difficulties in measuring the outcomes of intermediate treatment. These additional difficulties begin with the lack of accurate and relevant statistical information, the complexities of interpreting the data that does exist, and the trap of assuming that any links between attendance at an intermediate treatment project and changes in behaviour are causal.

One measure of re-offending is reconviction rates, and these are used to assess the effectiveness of custodial sentences. Thus, a commonly-quoted estimate is that more than eight in ten of those completing a youth custody order are reconvicted within two years, and around seven in ten of those who have served detention centre orders are reconvicted in the same period (see Curtis,1989; and Ball, in Doyle (ed.), 1989). Although there are no readily available national statistics, it seems to be commonly assumed – and indeed is an argument practitioners cite to promote community-based sentencing – that such sentences are at least as effective as custody as far as re-offending rates are concerned (see Knapp, in Kahan (ed.), 1989).

Reconviction rates are, however, a crude measure. There are well-documented hazards surrounding the interpretation of official statistics, including criminal statistics (see Box, 1971). Factors governing the content of criminal statistics include:

- the nature and levels of policing;
- the skill of offenders in evading detection;
- local arrangements which may affect how many cases proceed to caution or prosecution.

These points only hint at the likely deficiencies in re-offending data. During the research study, it became clear that the reporting of new offences to the police was itself a complex decision. Strong suspicion or hearsay that a young person had committed another offence was not, for example, thought sufficient proof on which to base a report to the police. At some centres – though not the case study centres – staff treat information about new offences disclosed during group meetings as confidential. At these centres, new offending behaviour is deemed to be dealt with via the normal programmes.

A further difficulty in evaluating the outcome of community-based interventions is that young people continue to be subject to a variety of influences – at home, at school, and in social contacts with their peer group. If offending ceases, it is hard to establish a causal relationship between this effect and attendance at an intermediate treatment centre. Motivation for the changed behaviour may have come from school, home or peer group – or may be attributable to increased maturity.

Yet another complicating factor is, as the three case studies will show, that programmes at intermediate treatment centres vary. Such differences can only be controlled for in large scale studies of intermediate treatment, when practitioners are able to specify their objectives, and when they are prepared to hold their methods of work constant.

It has already been stated that discouraging delinquent behaviour is not the only objective of intermediate treatment centres. At the case study centres, a second, major objective was to prevent unnecessary admissions to local authority care. In such care-related work, as well as in offence-related programmes, practitioners can have a range of more specific objectives. In the case study centres, specific objectives included:

- the provision of social education and life skills;
- encouraging personal growth;
- fostering constructive leisure pursuits;
- compensating for deprivation by providing enriching experiences.

The task of evaluating how effectively such specific objectives are achieved is not straightforward. The specific objectives being pursued with individual young people must be established and success criteria agreed. Yet practitioners may find it hard to delineate specific objectives, and agreed and validated measurement techniques may be lacking. While the researcher has the choice of a large number of psychological tests to evaluate personality development or attitude change, there still remains the problem of ensuring that measured changes can be securely attributed to the intermediate treatment programme. (For a more comprehensive discussion of these issues, see Downie and Ames, 1981.)

Again, experience during the fieldwork simply reinforced the issues raised here. For instance, achieving change is not always an objective of intermediate treatment programmes. The main objective of one programme observed was the provision of social education in a sympathetic forum. What would appropriate outcome measures be, whether:

- those involved attended regularly?
- they listened or contributed?

- they could remember the content of the discussions?
- at some future point in their lives, they based their actions on some guiding comments offered by the group leader?

A second lesson of the fieldwork was that some stated objectives can only be fulfilled as long as a young person is attending the project. Thus, constructive leisure pursuits, such as motorbike riding or banger racing, may only be available to a young person while he or she has access to the resources of an intermediate treatment centre. The centres' aim is to provide a legitimate means of pursuing an activity that their customers often pursue illegally. What the centres cannot provide is unlimited access to their facilities. Follow-up studies of these particular activities would, then, be unlikely to be fruitful.

How, then, was the problem of measuring outcome surmounted in this research programme? A 'solution' was sought in the approaches adopted in earlier evaluations of social programmes.

Contemporary history

The problems encountered in undertaking outcome studies in intermediate treatment, which have only been sketched in here, are common to much evaluative research in social science. A major obstacle to evaluating the results of social action projects has already been highlighted – that there is often only a very general level of agreement about objectives (*see* Ames, 1986). There can, therefore, be difficulties in establishing what counts as success. For that reason some social scientists have emphasised the primary importance of establishing exactly what is happening, certainly before attempting to measure any presumed outcomes. Indeed, it has been argued that establishing the facts of the matter is, in some sense, itself a form of evaluation.

In this research programme, the strategy adopted was to describe 'events' in the case study centres as accurately and completely as was feasible. This approach took into account the characteristics of social programmes already referred to. These are that they may not have well-defined objectives whose achievement – or otherwise – can be measured easily, and that the aims, and action taken to fulfil these, may well be subject to redefinition and revision in the light of practical experience. The research design in this programme tried to accommodate these realities, not ride roughshod over them.

The approach adopted has been called 'contemporary history'. Researching the American programmes against poverty in the 1960s, Marris and Rein argued:

'The whole process – the false starts, frustations, adaptions, the successive recasting of intentions, the detours and conflicts – needs to be comprehended. Only then can we understand what has been achieved, and learn from that experience. Research in this sense is contemporary history. Even though no one ever again will make exactly the same journey, to follow the adventures of the projects offers a general guide to the dangers and discoveries of their field of action. From such a guide, anyone may evaluate the experience according to his purpose.'(Marris and Rein, 1967, p.260)

The American research on poverty was designed to evaluate the outcomes of entirely new initiatives, but the emphasis on understanding processes seems highly pertinent in assessing continuing programmes too.

What intermediate treatment is and ought to be

Understanding and describing events in the case study centres is a necessary part of evaluating intermediate treatment. However, this is only the first step. Additionally, the research findings must be organised in a theoretical framework which helps to elucidate and to resolve key debates. Only then can the materials make a contribution to policy and practice.

One fundamental and continuing debate is about what intermediate treatment is and ought to be. The debate has persisted because – notwithstanding the efforts of a strong juvenile justice lobby in the 1980s – of the wide range of practice to be found under the umbrella of intermediate treatment. Examples abound. To give just one, the 'patchwork quilt' of provision was the starting point of an account of six intermediate treatment centres which was published in 1989. The centres reviewed covered the gamut of provision, from projects exclusively concerned with offering alternatives to custody, to a loosely knit confederation of informally run youth clubs, whose common objective was to help young people on the fringes of trouble. (Curtis, 1989)

Why has such a diversity of practice persisted in intermediate treatment? In this book, models of practice particularly prominent in intermediate treatment and in the work of the case study centres provide a basis for answering this question. The models will be used to disentangle the complex web of policy and practice that is intermediate treatment and to illustrate some of the recurring debates amongst policy makers and practitioners. What is most important is that these models help to clarify the variation in processes and outcomes of intermediate treatment encountered during the fieldwork and described in subsequent chapters.

The two models which have dominated discussion and analysis of intermediate treatment are those of 'justice' and 'welfare'. These models offer explanations of adolescent problems and suggest appropriate methods for dealing with them. In the 'justice' model, young people are thought to choose to offend. Two key strategies associated with this model are that any punishment should be proportional to the offence; and, that programmes of work with young offenders should focus on decisions about offending. The 'welfare' model defines young people in trouble or difficulties as vulnerable because of their disadvantaged environment. Relevant practice methods are to improve the young person's environment by, for example, intervening to prevent neglect and offering programmes that will alleviate the disadvantages experienced.

Particular premises of these two influential models have been highlighted and/or challenged by some analysts who, in turn, have proposed adapted approaches. The distinctive contributions of two alternative approaches will be considered alongside the 'justice' and 'welfare' models.

First is a 'developmental' approach which places particular stress on the transient nature of much juvenile offending. The suggested response of the approach to this relatively normal phase of development is to ensure that as many young people as possible are diverted from the juvenile justice system and that support and constructive opportunities are offered to them in their own communities. The second alternative approach defines key aspects of current arrangements for dealing with young offenders in terms of a 'corporatist' model. This approach does not offer an explanation of delinquency. Rather, it focuses attention on the issue that young offenders are increasingly processed administratively rather than judicially.

Conclusion

This chapter has described the research methods employed in this research programme, considered some of the problems associated with standard measures of outcome and suggested that the findings of the 'process' research – if organised within a theoretical framework – may make a valid contribution towards understanding outcomes. Before reporting on the study findings, the following chapter will discuss the policy and practice models in more detail, considering some of the research findings which support or refute each.

4. Theoretical perspectives

This chapter will discuss some theoretical approaches which offer differing interpretations of young people's problems and the methods for dealing with these. The two principal models to be discussed are those of 'welfare' and 'justice' (*see* Rutter and Giller, 1983; Parker, Sumner and Jarvis, 1989). The justice model has been especially influential in the last decade and, consequently, has been the focus of much critical attention. Scrutiny of this model has led some analysts to advocate alternative policies for dealing with young offenders and/or to highlight some consequences of current organisational arrangements. For example, there are the 'developmental' and 'corporatist' approaches (Rutherford, 1986; Pratt, 1989). Here, the intention is to outline the key ideas associated with each model or approach, to examine some research findings which support and test these ideas, and to consider some issues the models pose for practice.

The welfare model

The main tenets of the *'welfare'* model are, simply put, that delinquent and troubled adolescents are the products of deprived environments and that their problems can be tackled effectively through policies to combat neglect and disadvantage. As their problems are caused by adverse environments over which they have no control, young people should be regarded as less culpable than adults and more in need of care and protection. The policy response to delinquency and troublesome behaviour, linked to this model, has been to give discretionary powers to welfare agencies to provide more supportive environments.

Often closely aligned, or merged with the welfare perspective, is the *'treatment'* model. A distinction between the two is that the treatment perspective explains delinquency and disturbed behaviour, not in terms of external, environmental variables as in the welfare model, but as pathological conditions of individuals. The delinquency reflects deeper maladjustment, requiring diagnosis and treatment. As young people's needs are thought to vary, the practice implication is that flexibility and discretion are required in order to determine and implement appropriate methods of treatment. The discussion here focuses specifically on the welfare approach for, as will be seen, this approach was most evident to the researcher in the work of the case study centres.

What follows will seek to explain how the principles of the welfare model have been put into practice and with what consequences for young people. First of all, though, what is meant by a young person's 'environment' and, more precisely, what factors contribute to an adverse environment? A wide range of possible factors have been identified in the literature. In the immediate family environment, parental criminality, poor parental supervision, family discord and large family size are, with other variables, thought to be predictive of young people's problems. In the wider social environment, having a delinquent peer group and attending a school with a high proportion of less able or socially disadvantaged pupils, are included in a list of harmful influences. (West and Farrington, 1973)

The variety of environmental factors identified as having a potentially harmful effect explains why a broad range of programmes have been undertaken under the umbrella of 'welfare'. Such programmes have focused on individuals, families, particular institutions within localities – or even whole communities. Furthermore, the model's premises have encouraged practitioners to intervene to reduce the impact of disadvantage, even before any serious ill-effects have been observed. Such programmes, often described as 'preventive', have been offered to young people regarded as 'at risk'. Thus, a study undertaken in the mid-1980s identified the largest category of juveniles in intermediate treatment projects as those defined as 'at risk' (Harper and Thomas, cited by Morris and Giller, 1987), and two categories of the Cambridge researchers' typology of intermediate treatment, referred to in Chapter 1, are concerned primarily with 'preventive' work. (Bottoms and others, 1990)

The humane and caring impulses motivating practitioners to undertake preventive work are particularly well-illustrated in Holman's account of preventive 'community social work' on a Bath estate. Considerable personal and material costs can be incurred by practitioners committed to virtually open-ended involvement to improve the circumstances of young people's lives, attempting to avert them from getting into trouble (Holman, 1981). The issue to be addressed here, though, is what are the consequences of preventive intervention – that is work undertaken with vulnerable young people when problems are *predicted*, rather than irrefutably *confirmed*?

Logically, the first difficulty in evaluating preventive work would seem to be our ignorance of precisely what problems might have emerged had the work not been undertaken. Rutter and Giller suggest that there is reliable evidence about what social and family circumstances pre-dispose young people to delinquency. In fact the match between prediction and outcome seems good but by no means perfect. For example, Farrington's analysis of data from the Cambridge Study of Delinquent Development led him to conclude that 'potential offenders can be identified at an early age with a reasonable degree of accuracy' (Farrington, 1990). In this study, three-quarters of boys deemed 'vulnerable' at the age of eight were later convicted, with apparently only 30 per cent of the remainder being convicted.

Given that no prediction about offending will be entirely accurate, is there adequate justification for undertaking preventive programmes with young people deemed vulnerable? Rutter and Giller's viewpoint is that there is a general level of agreement in our society about the needs of young people and appropriate child rearing practices. The problem actually lies in the

'...considerable gap between identifying a damaging factor and knowing how to eliminate it or reduce its effect...The translation of general principles into effective policies of preventive action poses many unresolved problems, and we delude ourselves if we think that we have already obtained the answers. Regrettably, we have not.' (Rutter and Giller, 1983, p.324.)

This view, that the level of accuracy in targeting vulnerable populations is not matched by expertise in developing appropriate programmes, is not universally shared. Thus, evidence about the long-term effects of the American pre-school programme, Headstart, in improving cognitive ability and reducing delinquency, would support the value of preventive programmes (Farrington, 1985). It is helpful, therefore, to consider in a little more detail the kind of evidence on which Rutter and Giller and others have based their arguments, especially as these affect the work of intermediate treatment practitioners.

If the welfare model is correct in its assumptions about the adverse impact of environmental variables, a programme would be most likely to prevent delinquency if it can either remove harmful environmental factors, or neutralise their effects. In practice, it is beyond the scope of intermediate treatment to change environmental factors. What practitioners are able to do is to offer, for example, compensatory programmes of enriching activities, to help young people cope positively with their circumstances. These programmes may well have an intrinsic value, adding interest and excitement to young people's lives. But there is little evidence to suggest that activities such as a youth club might offer, which aim to occupy young people constructively, have any measurable impact on crime and delinquency. (Clarke, 1985; Rutter and Giller, 1983)

Another technique available to intermediate treatment practitioners is the counselling of young people, to encourage them to adopt acceptable lifestyles, or to provide them with techniques for dealing with problems they are experiencing, perhaps at school. Rutter and Giller suggest, however, tnat individual counselling has only limited impact while young people retain their other links with a high-risk environment. In other words, the positive outcomes of preventive work are likely to be limited by the powerful constraints of the wider environment.

Not only has it proved difficult to identify positive outcomes of preventive measures, the programmes have been argued to have negative consequences for young people. It has been suggested that, through their participation, young people acquire labels such as 'at risk' or 'pre-delinquent'. In addition to their negative impact on self-image, these labels may have the unintended consequence of drawing young people prematurely to the attention of law-enforcement and other official agencies – the so-called 'net-widening' effect. (*See* Young, 1971, Cohen 1972. And for a discussion of practitioners' beliefs about the labelling process, *see* Rogowski, 1990.)

The issue of net-widening is significant because it has been argued that early intervention in young people's lives can, should they later be caught offending, lead to unduly severe consequences. The Lancaster University researchers have warned:

'If the unlucky recipients of this pre-emptive supervision (unauthorised by any court and unspecified by any law) eventually do offend, in spite (or because) of all the efforts made on their behalf, they run the risk of being stigmatised almost as effectively in the social enquiry report of a disappointed social worker as they would be by a substantial record of previous convictions.' (Thorpe et al, 1980 p 39)

These fears, that preventive programmes can later cause a young person to receive an unwarrantedly 'high tariff', that is a severe court sentence, are grounded in evidence about the careers of young people in the care system. Being in the care of the local authority, including for preventive reasons, is known to have provided a 'fast lane' route to custody. (Thorpe, 1980; and, more recently, studies cited by the Prison Reform Trust, 1988)

How well substantiated, though, are concerns that attendance at an intermediate treatment centre for 'preventive' reasons may later lead to unduly severe sentencing? First, it is relevant to note that not all those attending a preventive programme will, at some later date, be charged with offending. As far as the proportion of young offenders vulnerable to the effects of 'net-widening' are concerned, one question is what reactions do magistrates have on learning about previous involvement in intermediate treatment? Direct evidence on this issue is hard to obtain. Their study of magistrates' decision-making in four urban areas led Parker and his colleagues to conclude that trying to anticipate the sentencing decisions of magistrates is a complex business:

'...we have been able to show that magistrates were influenced, in some way, by SERs in no fewer than 80 per cent of cases. However, when we unpack the contents of this influence a rather diverse picture emerges. This is because magistrates re-use the information provided to make moral assessments of offenders'. (Parker, Sumner and Jarvis, 1989)

Establishing the precise basis for magistrates' decisions is, then, not straightforward. It does seem clear, however, that information which may fuel magistrates' moral judgements would increase the severity of sentencing. The knowledge that a young person had experienced a community-based programme might sway magistrates' moral stance.

Seeking proof that early intermediate treatment involvement may later affect young people detrimentally is to examine only part of a wider issue. It has now been widely accepted that young people appearing in court should receive sentences appropriate to the severity of their offences. In the past, the adverse family circumstances and welfare of an offender have been found to influence magistrates to pass more severe sentences than might otherwise have been the case. Thus, government guidelines now require the authors of social enquiry reports to focus on offence-related information and to desist from automatic preparation of reports on first and second time offenders (Home Office Circular 17/83; Home Office Circular 92/86; DHSS, 1987). The experience of LAC(83) projects shows that this strategy helps to ensure offenders receive sentences low on the tariff of penalties – in practitioners' shorthand, they 'stay down-tariff'. When social enquiry reports were not submitted for first time offenders – unless specifically requested by the bench – the severity of sentences for first offenders decreased (*see*, for example, Warner, 1987). The implications of such findings have not, though, permeated all social work practice. Parker and his colleagues found that some social workers continued to include information about an offender's domestic circumstances, to demonstrate to the bench the case for welfare or social work intervention. (Parker, Sumner and Jarvis, 1989)

To sum up so far, preventive intermediate treatment has proved to be controversial. Opposition to it has been based in large part on the grounds that it has led to young people receiving unduly severe sentences if they subsequently appear in court. The evidence for this does not, however, appear beyond dispute. Some conclusions of Bottoms and the Cambridge research team usefully set the whole debate in perspective:

'The mechanism of possible up-tariffing effects from the use of preventive IT is easy to understand, and there is not much doubt that this process does sometimes occur. But the published empirical evidence for up-tariffing effects arising from preventive IT is surprisingly slight, given the impact that these alleged effects have had on IT policy in many local areas...It is also possible that up-tariffing effects can in any case be avoided...by various strategies such as the use of differing terminology...good SIR writing, the development of understanding with magistrates, good local systems management...The truth, which must not be obscured by the emotion which this topic sometimes generates, is that the key questions are empirical ones, and that our empirical knowledge in this area is at present inadequate.' (Bottoms and others, 1990, p 84)

Quite apart from the debate about exposing young people to the risk of receiving unwontedly severe sentences should they later appear in court, 'preventive' work – and work with those whose offences are too trivial to warrant a court appearance – is thought to raise important issues about safeguarding civil liberties. Preventive programmes are run at the discretion of practitioners. Morris and Giller highlight how petty offenders, who have been diverted to attend an intermediate treatment centre rather than appear in court, may be subject to pressure to admit their guilt, when available evidence might not be sufficient to prove guilt in a court of law. Those responsible for organising the programmes are not subject to formal scrutiny regarding, to take one example, their procedures for selecting who should attend. The programme itself may last longer and intrude more on personal freedom than would any court sentence for minor transgressions (*see* Morris and Giller, 1987).

An infringement of civil liberties is, then, implied which has to be considered alongside what is known about the benefits, or drawbacks, of the programmes. As the majority of young people committing trivial offences are indistinguishable from the mass of their contemporaries, it is not necessarily clear what 'treatment' should be pursued with them. Another possible disadvantage is the danger of contamination – that is, that the offending behaviour of petty offenders will escalate if they meet more experienced offenders at the intermediate treatment centre. (Rutter and Giller, 1983)

So far this discussion has tended to question the practice assumption of the welfare model, that social work intervention can counteract the adverse effects of a disadvantaged environment. Attention has been directed especially towards the possibility of ill-effects resulting from premature intervention and towards the implied intrusion on personal liberty. Intervention based on welfare principles is not, however, confined to preventive programmes. Compensatory, or enrichment, programmes have, for example, also been run for persistent offenders. How effective are such interventions?

Some welfare-oriented programmes have been found to have a measure of success with more persistent offenders – for example, well-planned and skilfully managed programmes offering social and vocational skills, and/or constructive leisure pursuits with a different peer group. But, whatever the degree of success, it remains the case that it has been found hard to sustain improvements in an unchanged environment. (Rutter and Giller, 1983)

More generally, Rutter and Giller point out that the welfare perspective largely ignores factors such as the seriousness of offences, the age at which offending began, and the range and frequency of offending. As these factors – as well as personality and familial variables – are important in predicting future offending, the effectiveness of the welfare approach is, arguably, limited, by its focus on the needs of the young person rather than his or her offending behaviour. (Rutter and Giller, 1983)

This discussion of the contribution and limitations of the welfare approach raises several issues for consideration in the case studies.

• Did any of the case study projects base their programmes on welfare principles?
• If so, how were welfare-oriented programmes viewed by those organising them and participating in them?
• Was there any evidence of 'net-widening' or the loss of civil freedoms?
• How did the staff of other agencies with whom the centres worked evaluate the approach?

Since completion of the fieldwork for this study, the debate about prevention has become more topical in the light of the provisions in the Children Act 1989 (referred to in Chapter 1) concerning local authorities' duties in the prevention of crime.

The justice model

In this model of practice, crime is perceived as a matter of opportunity and rational choice. Individuals are deemed responsible for their own actions and can, thus, be held accountable for their offending. Society's disapproval of lawbreaking can be demonstrated by the punishment of offenders; which serves not only as retribution but also to deter others. Punishment proportional to the offence is the 'just deserts' of the offender. The important contrast with the previous model is the denial of open-ended, discretionary and unaccountable interventions in the lives of young people.

How does this model inform practice in intermediate treatment? It was argued in Chapter 2 that much juvenile crime is petty.

Intermediate treatment practitioners who subscribe to the justice philosophy – or, as many prefer to be called, juvenile justice workers – seek, if at all possible, to keep young people out of court. Or, if young people are charged, to ensure that they receive community-based, rather than custodial sentences.

An important procedure practitioners employ to achieve these goals is the monitoring of social enquiry reports to ensure, for example, that proportionate, well-presented, community-based sentencing options are always available to the bench. In contrast to the welfare approach, where the length of intervention would in a sense depend upon practitioner judgements that rehabilitative goals have been achieved, 'justice' workers aim to offer clearly-defined, time-limited programmes.

An important emphasis in planned programmes for those fulfilling community-based sentences is likely to be the detailed examination of situations in which offending has taken place. Face-saving, non-delinquent responses, for use when opportunities and peer-group encouragement to offend occur, will be developed and rehearsed (*see* Thorpe, 1980; Denman, undated).

Another strand of practice in the justice model is the recording of local data – about offenders, their offences and the court sentences they receive. This data is collected to ascertain, for example, the characteristics of offences and offenders which appear to attract sentences high on the ladder of penalties. Unexpectedly severe sentences may be the subject of an enquiry to establish whether agreed practice was followed – whether, for example, a well-argued case for a lower-tariff alternative was included in the social enquiry report.

Projects operating according to the principles of the justice model have included those set-up under the LAC(83) initiative, of which one of the case study projects – North City – was one. The NACRO monitoring of these projects has provided detailed information about the level of success attained in reaching the goals of the model. The findings of the fourth census, which gave information about 65 of the 95 initiative projects in full operation in the study period, July to December 1986, suggested satisfactory implementation of targets (NACRO, 1987(a)). Thus, a significant drop in the numbers of juvenile offenders being prosecuted was noted. This national trend was thought to have been stimulated in local areas by the diversionary strategies introduced by the LAC(83) funded projects. Secondly, the projects were found to be successful in reducing the level of custodial disposals in their local courts. Between July and December 1985 and the same period in 1986, the rate of custodial sentences dropped from 9 per cent to just under 8 per cent, even though it was thought likely that the courts were dealing with fewer, but more serious and persistent offenders.

Furthermore, the total number of young people receiving either a care order, a custodial sentence, or a community-based sentence to complete at a LAC(83) centre, fell from 914 in the last six months of 1985, to 608 in the same period in 1986. The NACRO researchers concluded that effective 'gatekeeping' of the local juvenile justice sytems was being achieved, and that the increased numbers of offenders attending project programmes – 319 in the six-month study period, as compared with 236 in the equivalent period a year earlier – were actually those who would otherwise have received a custodial disposal. In the researchers' own words:

'The Fourth Census has produced remarkably good results "across the board". The right young people in greater numbers are being placed on schemes; care and custody for juveniles are being effectively eroded, programmes are being successfully completed, and all without any apparent "net-widening" effect.' (NACRO, 1987 (a), p.30)

The NACRO findings would, then, suggest that where justice-oriented schemes were established they were, in their own terms, successful. Some criticisms have, nonetheless, been directed at the justice model. Two, particularly pertinent to practice in intermediate treatment, have first questioned the power of social workers and juvenile justice workers to influence the delivery of justice and, secondly, expressed reservations about the value-orientation of the model.

Implementation of the justice model by social workers and juvenile justice workers assumes that these personnel have the power to influence decisions, initially, as to whether young people appear in court and, subsequently, about the sentencing outcome. The role of welfare professionals in diverting young people away from court appearances will be considered separately, in the review of the corporatist approach. To anticipate that discussion, it is clear that arrangements in at least some local authorities do empower practitioners to help divert young people from the courts. Some preliminary findings are cited, however, to query whether a simple policy of diversion automatically serves the interests of young people and their families. Considered now are some comments on the influence of practitioners on sentencing policy in the juvenile courts.

Several issues are raised in the literature. First, the government in power for the whole of the 1980s and into the 1990s was committed to policies of law and order, and sought to introduce tough penalties for offenders. Inasmuch as government policy was to punish offenders for what were regarded as freely chosen actions, its aims coincided with those of social workers and intermediate treatment practitioners who were seeking to limit the intervention in young people's lives to their 'just deserts'. The *ends* of both parties had some similarities. One of the means to this end pursued by the government was, however, to strengthen the power of the magistracy:

'Taken overall, the two Criminal Justice Acts of the 1980s represent something of a triumph for magistrates and may be taken as evidence of just how effective the Magistrates' Association is at parliamentary lobby. For juveniles in particular, the Acts have provided magistrates with a vast range of sentencing options. The new custodial powers together with compensation orders as a principal disposal, community service for 16-year-olds and 36-hour attendance centre orders, add up to an impressive array of punishment options. Indeed if the greater structure given by requirements in supervision and care orders is also seen as an extension of control, we have two key features in relation to juveniles: a much wider array of sentencing options and the potential for harsher punishments both custodial and non-custodial.' (Parker, Sumner and Jarvis, 1989, p.14)

This quotation suggests that the balance of power in the juvenile court rests squarely with the bench. Pitts, too, queries how dominant social workers and juvenile justice workers have been in the juvenile justice system. Some of the success of the justice approach in the 1980s may be attributed to the extent to which its objectives – albeit for quite different, ideological reasons – happened to accord with political objectives. Thus Pitts' analysis of the Lancaster University research team's delinquency management approach concluded

'They are on the side of the underdog offender and opposed to the professional systems heavyweights who stigmatise and imprison them. There is, as we have seen, a tendency in this analysis to locate the responsibility for all this injustice with low-level operatives...the delinquency management perspective largely confines itself to an analysis of the functioning of local authority social services departments and is silent on the issue of penal provision...The growing popularity of delinquency management is in large part attributable to the worsening economic situation and the financial constraints in which local authorities currently operate. As a pragmatic approach it remains unreflective about the roots of its own strategies and uncritical of an increasingly authoritarian response to young offenders by governments throughout the 1970s and 1980s.' (Pitts, 1988, p.87)

Contrasted with the evidence presented by NACRO, the analyses of Pitt and Parker raise some empirical questions about the influence which social workers and juvenile justice workers *can* exert over magistrates.

The relative power of the welfare professionals has also been put into question by data about how accurately social workers and juvenile justice workers have been able to read the bench and negotiate the least punitive sentence. Parker's study of magistrates' sentencing showed that social enquiry reports recommended alternatives to custody in a proportion of cases not perceived by the bench as at real risk of custody. In three of the courts studied such 'slippage' was judged to be 'considerable, with report writers seeing their primary task to divert cases from custody when magistrates saw no case for custody in the first place.' (Parker, Sumner and Jarvis, 1989)

Another insight into the relative power of the bench and social work and juvenile justice practitioners has been provided by evidence about the importance magistrates have assigned to school reports. Such reports have not always been made available to parents and defendants (Ball, 1983) nor challenges over the truth of their contents fruitful (Parker, Sumner and Jarvis, 1989). Yet school reports, when available, have been found greatly to influence sentencing decisions, as magistrates believed them

'...to be objective and reliable assessments of defendants' characters. This contrasted with their suspicions that social enquiry reports were often biased and unrealistic documents.' (Parker, Sumner and Jarvis, 1989, p.135)

Parker found that whilst school reports were not always available on his sample – they were available for 59 out of 120 juveniles – they were perhaps the only report available on those at an early stage in their offending career, and for whom social workers had therefore not prepared a social enquiry report. Magistrates' reliance on the truthfulness of school reports was unfounded, for:

'...there was a depressing similarity in terms of content, with a preponderance of extremely judgemental and negative observations under every heading...frequently without any substantiating evidence.' (Parker, Sumner and Jarvis, 1989, p.137)

Despite their unproven basis, Parker and his team found that such reports tended to push those on whom they were written 'up-tariff'. The power and influence of social workers and intermediate treatment practitioners in implementing delinquency management techniques would seem, then, to be somewhat contested.

The second debate reviewed here is about the values contained in the justice model. These have been challenged by those who regard it as unjust that all young offenders should be regarded as equally culpable. Some commentators, recognising that justifiable criticisms have been made of both pure welfare and pure justice approaches, have argued for a balance of justice *and* welfare (*see*, for example, Parsloe, 1976; Harris, 1985).

Parsloe and Harris argue that both needs and rights should be incorporated in the criminal justice system. An over-emphasis on welfare issues is known to have put individual rights at risk and the Gault case in the USA is quoted as evidence of this. The Gault case involved a juvenile being ordered to be imprisoned until he came of age for an offence punishable, for an adult, by a fine or two months' imprisonment. But in turn, Parsloe argues, the dominance of justice principles can mean insufficient attention being paid to people's 'needs'. Parsloe reconciles the dilemma by suggesting that particular emphasis be paid to 'confining, structuring and checking' social workers' discretion through, for example, the use of contracts agreed by social workers and clients.

Harris also focuses upon the case for controlling welfare interventions. He, too, notes that the net result of the welfare elements in the 1969 Children and Young Persons Act was an increased number of young offenders being removed from their homes. Yet he, too, records the view that justice needs tempering with welfare

'...a philosophy of justice which jettisons a range of humanising values such as compassion, tolerance, altruism and a quest for social justice...is removing from its scope the capacity to act with wisdom as well as justice.' (Harris, 1985 p 37)

Harris favours what he terms 'just welfare' which can, he argues, be incorporated in the design of a juvenile justice system such that it:

'...acknowledges both the personal and social need apparent in some (though not all) young offenders, and also the obligation of the state to provide a justice system which punishes illegal behaviour.' (Ibid p 32)

One key to this is for welfare intervention, like formal justice, to:

'...be limited by the nature of the offence, and that the additional involvement of welfare professionals should be entirely voluntary, outside the normal court-based functions of the social worker, and actively requested by the client...[to achieve this a] sentencing principle of limiting welfare seems necessary.' (Ibid, p 39)

Thus, in the estimation of Harris, welfare issues are a legitimate concern of the courts but only if intervention is limited in proportion to the offence.

Proposals for a system which combines justice and welfare principles have themselves been criticised (*see* Morris and Giller, 1987). The grounds for criticism are, first, that justice theorists have not denied that young offenders may have 'needs' to which social work help may be an appropriate response. But, secondly, that juveniles should not be *sentenced* to social work. Social work services should certainly be made available but by channels other than the juvenile justice system, which has a poor record as far as delivering welfare services is concerned.

What questions does the justice standpoint pose for this study? Where practitioners claim adherence to justice principles, it will be relevant to consider how programmes are managed, for example:

• Is there greater emphasis on the exact length of programmes?
• Is the content of programmes more carefully targeted towards dealing with the context and situation of crimes?
• Are welfare issues acknowledged and resolved?
• How effective do attempts to manage the juvenile justice system appear to be?

These issues are amongst those addressed in the chapters on the case studies.

The welfare and justice models represent the two principal approaches to understanding and dealing with young offenders and other young people in difficulties. The debate between them is longstanding and well pre-dates the 1980s pro-justice resurgence. These two views do not, however, encompass all strands of thinking pertinent to an understanding of how the problems of young people have been, or might be, handled. To support their contention that punishment of young offenders should not be disproportionate to their crimes, proponents of the justice model have pointed to evidence that most young people grow out of offending. The view that offending can be deemed a developmental, rather than a criminal, concern is the starting point for what Rutherford has called a 'developmental' approach.

Developmental issues

The primary objective of the developmental perspective is that young people with problems should be enabled to remain in their communities. Practitioners should seek 'to strengthen the commitment and capacity of home and school to hold on to young people' (Rutherford, 1986). This approach is, again, based on an interpretation of the research evidence:

- that much adolescent offending behaviour is petty;
- that most young people grow out of offending – although the peak age for offending for young males has risen to 18 years (HMSO,1988);
- that since it is hard to distinguish known offenders from many of their contemporaries, there is little justification for subjecting them to court procedures and punishments whose beneficial effects are largely unproven.

Evidence for each of these presumptions has already been discussed.

Those implementing a justice model also cite evidence about the transitional nature of offending, in support of their strategies of diversion. Distinctive to the developmental model is its practice lesson that greater reliance should be placed upon homes, schools and communities to support and manage young people during their difficult adolescent years. For, it is suggested, young people have a better chance of learning to be mature and responsible adults in their own homes and communities than in the so-called universities of crime – custodial institutions. Discussion here centres on how this policy would be accomplished and what this might mean for young people.

The proposals of the main protagonist of the approach, Rutherford, for achieving these aims start with the option of offering assistance to families, to help them fulfil their responsibilities for dealing with difficult members. Such help could range from easing the economic and care burdens of families – by enhancing child benefits or providing additional day care facilities – to offering specialised family counselling services. Schools, too, would be encouraged to hold on to troublesome pupils longer through provisions to improve their pastoral role. Specific changes would be an increase in resources, specialist training of teachers and the availability of other specialists to support staff in schools. Outside schools, unemployed adults are identified as a vulnerable group for whom mutual support groups might be a valuable community-based lifeline.

Rutherford's other proposals relate to the management of the juvenile justice system. In this context the work of Basingstoke's Woodlands Centre is referred to approvingly:

'It was within community placements that the most significant changes have occurred. Growing from a crude notion of using voluntary help and effecting indirect reparation, the placements now encourage the local community to take an interest in, and indeed, 'manage' the delinquents within their area. Obviously, this requires support, encouragement and supervision from the Centre, but we have been encouraged by the positive response shown by local communities in dealing with their young offenders...' (Owen, 1984; quoted by Rutherford, 1986, p 141)

Rutherford's message, that the developmental approach is best for young people, is convincingly conveyed, and includes clear warnings about avoiding the dangers of net-widening. Yet the lessons learned from the implementation of other models point to some controversial issues, for example:

● How would members of the community be selected to work with offenders?
● How much discretion would they be allowed to exercise in dealing with troublesome young people?
● When and how would intervention be terminated?
● Might there be problems associated with confidentiality of information about young people?

Underpinning all these questions is the possibility that undue intrusion in, and control over, the lives of young people might result from the strategies outlined above.

Another account of how delinquency may be dealt with in the community puts these critical questions into sharper focus. Hoghughi (1983) has also advocated transferring some power and resposibility away from experts onto lay persons. He has argued '...crime affects everyone, and is everyone's responsibility'. Like Rutherford, Hoghughi examines the role of parents, peers and schools. Thus, parents should not suffer the removal of their children on 'welfare' grounds, except as a last resort, but be helped to control their children. Peer groups should be supported in constructive leisure pursuits and, perhaps with the aid of incentive schemes, encouraged to engage in mutual dissuasion from offending. In their curricula, or extra-curricula programmes, schools should emphasise socially acceptable behaviour patterns and the development of self-control. Furthermore, schools could be made to take responsibility for truancy and delinquent behaviour which in a sense they can be said to generate. They could also be required to elaborate on what ways they are acting to combat the problems. As far as community solutions for social problems and delinquency are concerned, Hoghughi has proposed:

'Members of a visible and mutually known neighbourhood or other locally demarcated area must assume responsibility for their youngsters and other problem people in their midst.' (Hoghughi, 1983 p 287)

Economic incentives to do so would be made available. Hoghughi envisaged that these measures of increased community control would be implemented alongside other methods of treatment and punishment of young offenders.

The slant of Hoghughi's proposals, suggested by his title *The Delinquent, Directions for Social Control*, highlights some of the practice dilemmas posed by his approach. In particular, Hoghughi's assumption that schools, peer groups and neighbourhoods can bear responsibility for the problems caused by their members raises doubts as to whether this may lead to a variation on the process of blaming the victim (Ryan, 1971). It cannot be assumed that schools and local communities condone all that occurs in them, nor that efforts have not been made to combat the problems. The problems may be too large for them to tackle, or their 'solutions' unacceptable to the wider society.

The proposals outlined above accord with a trend noted by various analysts (*see* Pratt, 1985) for more aspects of young people's lives to be subjected to some form of assessment. Associated with such scrutiny, whether open or hidden, is a broadening of groups deemed 'at risk' and requiring some kind of community support – for example the young unemployed – and the sharing of information, not necessarily verified, between collaborating agencies. Scrupulous practice is required to avoid any adverse consequences. (Pratt, 1985)

Questions posed in relation to these developmental strategies are as follows.

• Has the developmental approach influenced practice at the case study centres? If so, in what practical ways has it been implemented?
• Which groups of young people have been included in relevant programmes and on what grounds?
• Have methods adopted successfully reflected the humanitarian concerns of the model, that young people should be enabled and supported to remain in their own communities?
• Has intervention been proportional to the problems defined?

The case study accounts offer some insights into these issues and conclusions are drawn in the concluding chapters of the book.

Justice or corporatism?

The final perspective considered here, corporatism, shifts attention away from the causes of delinquency. It examines features of current methods for dealing with young offenders and questions whether these arrangements further the objectives of the justice model, as is intended. In his analysis, Pratt has argued that the administration of juvenile justice is better described in terms of corporatism than justice. (Pratt, 1989)

The focus of the corporatist model is clearly somewhat different from the three approaches discussed so far. Corporatism does not offer an explanation of delinquency and suggest appropriate practice solutions. Rather, it offers an analytical framework for an accurate understanding of juvenile justice policy and practice in the 1980s. (Pratt 1989)

As we enter the 1990s, the key features of practice whose effects are here the subject of debate include:

'an increase in cautioning: the single most important sanction for juvenile offenders is the police caution.

a growth of inter-agency co-operation, to achieve more effective and efficient sentencing policies and to establish crime prevention schemes. An example of the former is the setting-up of panels to agree sentencing recommendations to the courts.

the development of a wide range of community-based, alternative to care and custody programmes.

a reduction of 'professional' autonomy in some areas: for example, courts are restricted in their use of custody by the restrictive clauses in the 1982 and 1988 Criminal Justice Acts; social work referrals to community-based programmes are limited in some areas to those being diverted from court or custody, or who meet other, stated criteria; the authors of social enquiry reports have often to conform to certain formulae in their report-writing.

the voluntary sector's role in the provision of intermediate treatment has been enhanced, especially via the LAC(83) initiative.

the development and use of information technology to assist delinquency management.

a trend towards 'bifurcation': that is, drawing a distinction between dangerous, 'hard core' offenders, for whom custody could be required, and less serious offenders for whom community-based measures are appropriate.' (Pratt, 1989)

In summary, in the 1980s juvenile justice practice demonstrated:

'an increase in administrative decision-making, greater sentencing diversity, involvement of non-juridical agencies, and high levels of containment and control in some sentencing programmes.' (Pratt, 1989)

It is Pratt's contention that these significant trends were 'necessary and essential features of a third model of juvenile justice: corporatism' (Pratt, 1989).

This term refers, essentially, to the removal or management of conflict via cooperation between professional and interest groups, and by their agreement on common aims and objectives.

In contrast, Pratt suggests, important features of the justice model – 'certainty, due process, visibility, accountability, least restrictive intervention' – were not as evident in current juvenile justice practice. His general conclusion is that the justice/welfare debate could not account for all that has occurred in delinquency management in the 1980s.

An organisation which has exhibited some of the features of corporatism described by Pratt is the Northampton Juvenile Liaison Bureau. The Bureau, established by merging various agencies concerned with young people, aimed to divert the majority of young offenders from the courts. A description of the work of this agency has highlighted aspects of administrative decision-making and delivery of 'justice'. (Davis, Boucherat and Watson, 1989)

The Bureau has sought to achieve its objectives, of diverting young people from prosecution and other kinds of formal intervention, through the creation of a range of low-level, informal procedures, such as informal warnings. A small-scale study of how this approach worked in practice revealed, amongst other findings, that there was disagreement amongst Bureau staff as to the appropriate action in any case. Such disagreement was, at least partly, related to the backgrounds of staff. In particular, the police representatives at the Bureau were likely to argue for more substantial intervention, than were social work or probation staff. The latter staff's views were, though, more influential in the Bureau. (Davis, Boucherat and Watson, 1989)

The study authors found that the desire to avoid formal intervention, so as to avoid removing young people from their existing social networks, was not necessarily accompanied by efforts to ascertain what the existing networks were. Nor, where control was lacking, were attempts made to resolve that circumstance. Indeed, even where parents appeared to be seeking official intervention, including the prosecution of their child, Bureau staff did not ensure that some kind of assistance was made available to the family. The authors of this study argued, in effect, that in certain respects the juvenile courts offered a better service than the Bureau:

'that there are certain criteria – most obviously, visibility and accountability – against which the JLB suffers in comparison with the juvenile court. If nothing else, our observations confirm that administrative decision-making by police and social workers cannot offer...a form of 'local tribunal', responsive to victim and offender perspectives and reflecting neighbourhood justice norms.' (Davis, Boucherat and Watson, 1989, p.234)

The questions which this very brief introduction to corporatism raises for this study include:

• Is this perspective applicable in describing and analysing arrangements for the management of young offenders in the case study centres?
• Where inter-agency collaboration occurs, how are different perspectives reconciled?
• How are the wishes and needs of young people and their families acknowledged and dealt with?

Conclusion

This chapter has considered the two dominant models of practice in the management of young people in trouble – justice and welfare. It has also described two further perspectives – developmental and corporatist – which have emerged in debates about juvenile justice. Following descriptions of the case study centres in the three following chapters, we will return to these models and perspectives to assess their applicability to the work of the centres.

5. North City, Liverpool

The North City Centre was established in 1986 with funding under the (then) Department of Health and Social Security's LAC(83) initiative. This finance was for the development of intensive intermediate treatment programmes for young people who would otherwise receive custodial sentences from the courts. In January 1985 Barnardo's, with the sponsorship of Liverpool's social services department, received DHSS approval for its application for an intermediate treatment centre in the north of the city (Craig, 1985). Difficulties in obtaining suitable premises accounted for the delay before the Project started work in January 1986.

Aims and objectives

The work of the North City Project reflected the requirements of the DHSS LAC(83) circular and the philosophy of the staff at the Project during the research. The particular aims of the Project, as given in its 1986 and 1987 annual reports, were

'The primary aim of the Project is to provide credible community alternatives to care and custody for young offenders between the ages of 10 and 17 years.

The secondary aim is to ensure monitoring of the juvenile justice system to check areas of need, the effects of intervention and possible ways of influencing local practice.

We believe that, except where there is a recognised need for care, community-based provision for juvenile offenders is preferable to removal from home and placement in an institution.'

The entire focus of the North City Project was, then, on offering and promoting the provision of alternatives to custody for young offenders.

The building

The Project was based in a terraced house, rented from a local community association. Downstairs, there was a large, open-plan room, part of which housed a (much used) snooker table; the other part of which was a sitting area, furnished with comfortable chairs. Also downstairs were a well-fitted, modern kitchen and a small secretarial office. Upstairs, there were two offices and a small conference/meeting room. The house was well-decorated and well-maintained. It was carpeted throughout. Overall, the accommodation for the Project was clean, comfortable and remarkably cosy, given the numbers of young people and adults who used the building. The exterior of the Project building differed from the other houses in the street inasmuch as there were wire grills over the windows. At the back of the house there was a yard, with a shed for housing wood and other materials.

The area served by the Project

North City Intermediate Treatment Project served a social services district to the north of Liverpool's city centre. The 1985 population estimates suggested a population of just under 59,000 in this district – nearly 12 per cent of the city's population. This figure may have been a slight under-estimate of the 1989 population, for, while the population of Liverpool has been declining in recent years, there has been a significant amount of new house building in North City.

In 1989, there were nine social services districts in Liverpool. Available socio-economic data suggest that, given its share of the city's population, the area covered by the North City Project had slightly fewer social problems in comparison with the city as a whole. The district had around:

- nine per cent (852) of the city's overcrowded households;
- ten per cent (4,398) of those economically active and seeking work;
- eight per cent (102) of the number of children in care in the city;
- seven per cent (5,036) of the city's council houses;
- eight per cent (400) of the city's lone parent with children households.

Juvenile justice work in North City

The numbers of young people from the Project's patch who, in 1988, were sentenced in the courts were broadly in proportion to the district's share of the population. Thus, approximately 11 per cent of the city's juvenile justice work was with young people from North City (that is, work undertaken on 87 cases) (Copp et al., 1988).

What is clear (though the numbers were admittedly small) is that, absolutely and proportionately, young people from this district appearing before the courts were more likely in 1988 to receive a sentence including a requirement of intermediate treatment than were young people from other districts. Nearly a quarter (11) of the 48 orders including intermediate treatment given by the courts in 1988 were to young people from North City. Looked at another way, just about one in *eight* of the main sentences passed on young people from North City included an intermediate treatment requirement. However, only one in *17* of the main sentences passed on young people from other areas of the city included an intermediate treatment requirement.

One possible explanation for the higher incidence of sentences including intermediate treatment in North City could be use of this requirement for minor offences, for which lower tariff sentences might have been appropriate. The higher numbers of orders including intermediate treatment requirements in the district did not, however, seem to be at the expense of outcomes lower on the tariff. To use a crude measure, nearly eight in ten (78 per cent) of main sentences passed on young people from the district were lower on the tariff than an intermediate treatment requirement. This proportion of, relatively, lower tariff sentences was not dissimilar to the average for other social services districts in the city (76 per cent). The proportion of high tariff, youth custody and detention centre sentences in the district was, consequently, *lower* than in other districts. These two sentences (youth custody and detention centre sentences) formed only two per cent of sentences given to young people from the North City, the lowest proportion of such sentences for any social services district. Comparative figures for other districts showed anything between five and fourteen per cent of sentences as being for youth custody or detention centre. The Project staff believed that the relatively high proportion of community-based sentences passed on young people from their district could be attributed to their procedures, which were consistently applied, for monitoring young people at risk of custody and intervening on their behalf.

Project staff

The staffing complement for the Project during the study was three full-time and two part-time employees. The full-time staff were the Project leader and two Project staff; the part-time staff were a clerk/typist and a cleaner/caretaker.

The Project leader was a qualified social worker. Immediately prior to joining Barnardo's, she had worked in intermediate treatment in a local authority team in another city. One Project worker was also a qualified social worker. For six years prior to joining the North City Project, he had worked in a specialist delinquency team in a social services district in the south of the city. In this post he had worked closely with the Barnardo's Intermediate Treatment Centre in Speke. The second Project worker was a temporary appointee, replacing a permanent Project worker who was on long-term sick leave. The temporary worker had previously been a volunteer at the Project. During the study, he obtained a place on a CQSW course at a polytechnic in the region, to start the following autumn.

The volunteers

At the time of the fieldwork, there were five volunteers working at the Project. The main responsibility for three volunteers was running an activity session, one evening each week, when young people at the Project were introduced to a range of acceptable leisure pursuits in the community. One of these volunteers was also a driver of the Project's minibus. The fourth volunteer worked mainly with young people who attended the Project following a police caution. The final volunteer had had extensive involvement with the Project, including a stint as temporary Project worker. During the study her main task was undertaking home visits to young people who were being considered for a caution.

Workload at the project

Three main sources of information about the workload of the Project were available to the researcher:

- city-wide statistics about juvenile justice in Liverpool;
- the annual reports which the Project had published; and
- the Project's own records.

The Liverpool Juvenile Justice Monitoring System statistics aimed to monitor crime and sentencing trends across the city for all Liverpool juveniles who appeared in court (Copp et al, 1987, 1988). These data showed that during 1987, nine juveniles living in North City were given sentences of a supervision order with intermediate treatment requirements, and a further two juveniles were given sentences of supervision orders with supervised activity requirements. During 1988, the corresponding figures were of 11 juveniles with intermediate treatment requirements and one with a supervised activity requirement.

These summary statistics were actually collated by two staff in the North City Team, a project worker and the secretary, in collaboration with the principal officer for intermediate treatment in the local authority. This allocation of limited staff resources reflected the commitment of the Project to their gatekeeping role, to prevent juveniles going into custody or care.

The monitoring statistics were valuable in presenting a broad picture of juvenile justice in the city of Liverpool. Their design for this purpose, however, resulted in their depicting only a limited view of the work of the Project. They did not include, for example, work undertaken with young people who had received a police caution, those on bail support programmes, or those on after-care programmes. There were also some young people from other districts who undertook their supervised activity order requirements in the North City Project.

The second source of information, the annual reports, detailed the Project's entire workload. In 1987, the Project worked with, in total, 45 young people. Of these, seven were police cautions, five were on bail support, nine were on supervision orders with intermediate treatment requirements, eight were on supervision orders with supervised activity requirements and six attended the Project for after-care. Assessment and court work was undertaken with ten young people who subsequently received custodial sentences. (*See* Table 5.1.)

A third source of information about the Project's workload was the data held at the Project. The main records held at the Project included individual files for each young person who attended the Project as part of a community based sentence or bail support programme. These files detailed the offence records of young people, their court appearances and sentences, their attendances at the Project and the 'work' that they had undertaken at the Project. Copies of court reports and correspondence were included in these files. Project staff also recorded in the file any particular problems they had encountered in dealing with the young person, along with details of any action taken over these – such as the sending of a warning letter following non-attendance. The case files were the most comprehensive records held by the Project.

Table 5.1 Workload at North City

	1987	*1988*
Police cautions	7	13
Bail support	5	1
Supervision order with intermediate treatment requirement	9	11
Supervision order with supervised activity requirement	8	5
After-care	6	_*
Assessment and court work	10	7
Total	45	37

*Those young people who attended the Centre for after-care in 1988, following completion of their sentence, are classified according to the sentence they received.

Other recording systems provided outline information on young people discussed at juvenile and cautioning panels. Thus, in January 1989, a separate record was established of the names, agreed recommendations and sentences passed on those discussed at juvenile panels. A card index recorded the names and ages of those considered at the cautioning panel, together with the recommendations made by the panel. A newer cautioning book, started in January 1989, also recorded whether the cautioning panel recommendation was subsequently accepted by the police and the nature of any intermediate treatment follow-up work. Finally, a record book was kept of all sentences received by young people in the district.

Examination of these data sources suggested that during 1988 the Project worked with a total of 37 young people. The amount and type of work varied. (*See* Table 5.1.) Eleven young people attended the Project to fulfil the requirements of an intermediate treatment order and five to fulfil supervised activity requirements. Of those on supervised activity orders, four were referred from other local authority intermediate treatment centres in the city.

The main point to note about the workload associated with administering an order is that it often extended beyond the formal intermediate treatment or supervised activity programme. Thus, the Project staff may, additionally, have been involved in one or more of the following:

- assessment prior to a court hearing to judge whether a young person was likely to cooperate with the Project staff in a community based programme;
- preparation of reports for the court;
- provision of a bail support programme;
- provision of an after-care programme to some of those still on supervision orders after the completion of their intermediate treatment orders.

If and when young people re-offended, Project staff were likely to recommence this cycle of work. For example, of the 16 young men sentenced by the courts to attend the Project in 1988, one also attended a bail support programme during that year, four attended the Project for informal assessment prior to a further court hearing and one attended, at different times, for both informal assessment and bail support.

In addition to work with this core of 16 young people, the Project staff wrote reports for the courts on five young people (three from North City and two from other districts in the city) who received sentences that did not include intermediate treatment or supervised activity requirements. Long-term bail support was offered to one young man, and two young people attended the Project for informal assessment.

The final strand of work with young people during 1988 was with the 13 young people who were considered at the cautioning panel. Project staff undertook a home visit for each of these young people in order to make a verbal report to the panel. At the panel, agreement was reached that 12 should be recommended for a police caution and, of these, that 11 should also attend the Project for follow-up sessions. The decision of the cautioning panel was not recorded for the last case.

One general point that can be made about the systems for recording workload at the Project, was that the choice of recording methods was consistent with the philosophy and orientation of the Project staff in their dealings with young people. This match between the objectives of the Project staff and the recording procedures was evident in various ways.

First, the Project staff elected to produce the city's juvenile justice monitoring statistics. This choice was rooted, it seems, in the complete commitment of Project staff to a justice model or systems approach to the management of juvenile offenders – that is an approach advocating the minimum of legal and welfare interventions in the lives of young people. The city's monitoring system was an important element in this strategy for juvenile justice systems management, as knowledge of crime and sentencing trends in the city enabled practitioners to plan services and responses.

Secondly, no common or 'group' records were held at the Project, of attendance at sessions. All information collected pertained to individuals. More will be said later about the work that was undertaken with young people – the relevant point here is that the Project was not attempting to run groups but to work *individually* with young people. The recording system was organised accordingly.

Thirdly, there was an awareness in the Project of the civil liberties of young people, evident in the desire not to record more information than was warranted about young people and in expressed concerns about the researcher seeking access to case files.

The weekly routine

Young people who were on supervision orders with an intermediate treatment clause were required to attend the Project three evenings (Monday, Tuesday and Wednesday) each week. The programme for these evening sessions was described in reports to the court in the following terms:

'[Monday] Individual work sessions, designed to rigorously challenge established delinquent attitudes and subsequently to encourage and enable the young person to follow a more socially acceptable lifestyle in the community.

[Tuesday] Social and life skills training, planned to take account of those areas in the young person's life where difficulties are being experienced.

[Wednesday] Structured leisure activities, which can be continued after the completion of the programme. The aim is to introduce the young person to local community facilities.'

Young people with supervised activity requirements attended these three evening sessions but also came to the Project to report to staff on Friday evenings and for a reparation session on Saturday mornings. Thursday evenings were reserved for those who were attending the Project following a police caution. The Project was normally closed between Saturday lunch-time and Monday morning. On occasional weekends, staff took young people away for a weekend, or volunteers would accompany young people on a leisure activity. During the study, young people had opportunities to spend a weekend in a cottage in Wales, to participate in a canoeing course and to go on a motor safari.

To return to the beginning of the week; how were the main sessions of the intermediate treatment and supervised activity order programmes organised? On Monday and Tuesday evenings, young people started arriving at the Project around 4 p.m. and stayed until the Project closed, at between 7 and 7.15 p.m. First to arrive were those still of school age. Those who were employed, generally on training schemes, arrived after work, an hour or so later. A fixed point of these evenings was a work component, which might be undertaken by staff with individual young people or might be organised as a group activity. From the material held in individual records, and from observations during the study, it was evident that this work component was often a written exercise. For example, on Monday evenings, the exercises designed to challenge and confront offending included questionnaires on personal beliefs about values and crime, and on images of the police. Alternatively, more factual quizzes about crime on Merseyside, about the rights of individuals as defined in the Police and Criminal Evidence Act or, more generally, about the rights of those taken into care or custody were set. Over a series of weeks during the study, the staff used adaptations of Denman's exercises, designed to elicit information both about the situational context of offences committed by young people at the Project – when they occurred, where, with whom, why – and about the young people's reactions to their offending – then and now. Information derived from these exercises informed Project staff about the values, attitudes and behaviour of the young people outside the Project and provided a starting point for discussions about future behaviour. (Denman, n.d.)

On Tuesday evenings, the social skills exercises could be practical or written. Shortly before the study, for example, several sessions were organised around the theme of living independently on limited means. Meals were planned and food for them bought and prepared at the Project. Skills such as ironing clothes were practised. Written work included job hunting, job application and money management exercises, and quizzes on issues such as drinking and driving. These exercises all had a clear relevance to the circumstances of young people at the Project and were designed to help them cope with situations they were, or would be, facing.

Progress through these more formal aspects of the Project's programmes was on an individual basis. The expectation, quite rigorously enforced, was that young people would start their intermediate treatment or supervised activity programmes on the evening of the day that the sentence was passed in court. During their time at the Project, young people were expected to complete a range of formal work sessions of the type described. But there was no set progression through the programme – a start was made with the work planned for everyone that same evening. This rolling pro-gramme approach did present some practical difficulties for staff, in knowing who had done what. To provide an easy reference guide, a summary sheet listing the exercises each young person had com-pleted was introduced during the study and was filed with the individual's records. This new recording procedure served to provide a partial answer to the periodic staff questions of 'What shall we do tonight?' and 'How many have, or have not, done that already?'

The amount and quality of written work completed by young people at the Project varied quite considerably. What individuals had done depended on how long they had attended the Project; their ability to complete the work; and their attitude to such exercises. It should be noted here that, collectively, young people attending the

Project certainly tackled a significant amount of formal and practical work on offending and on life skills.

The expectation of staff at the Project was that the young people would do whatever work was asked of them. If the required formal work was not completed on a Monday evening, the young person was expected to complete it on arrival at the Project on Tuesday.

The detailed consideration here of the formal elements of the Project's programmes reflects their centrality in presenting the Project's work to outside agencies, especially to the courts. Yet, the work sessions took up only a small proportion of each young person's Monday and Tuesday evenings at the Project, perhaps an average of 15 to 20 minutes. For the remainder of these evenings, most young people would chat and play snooker. Alternatively, if there was more than one adult in the Project, staff member or volunteer, games were set up on the Project's BBC computer, which was housed in the staff office. A focal point of the evening was the snack supper, which was frequently the house speciality – vegetable and ham soup. During the evening, staff would talk informally to young people and perhaps chase up non-attenders. The amount of contact between staff and young people depended, inevitably, on the numbers of adults present. On several evenings during the study, when members of staff were on sick leave or on a course, the evening session was run by one member of staff. He or she was likely to be helped by at least one volunteer for part of the evening. The volunteers could not, though, generally reach the Project until after the end of their working day and were not always able to be present.

The organisation of the week's programme was such that, at least for those fulfilling intermediate treatment requirements, the week's formal work was completed before the Wednesday activity evening. It was not the case that participation in the Wednesday evening activity was dependent on attendance and cooperation earlier in the week. The activity evening was viewed, rather, as an important element in the programme in its own right. As already noted, the activity evening was run by volunteers. Its purpose was to introduce young people to legitimate and acceptable ways of spending leisure time in the local community. Activities offered around the time of the study included visits to a local snooker hall, a staff versus young people football match, and a theatre visit.

The distinction between the intermediate treatment and higher-tariff, supervised activity programmes was that the latter was more intensive and included a reparative element. Thus, only the young people on supervised activity orders were required to report to staff at the Project on Friday evenings. Although they had only to 'report in', the young people often spent some time at the Project, talking and playing snooker.

The reparative element of the supervised activity programme took place on Saturday mornings. During the study this session was supervised by the temporary Project worker. The work undertaken included the making of fire surrounds for sale, and minor building jobs and repairs at the Project – such as the building of shelves or the repair of the stair bannister. The scale of what could be undertaken was limited by the space and facilities available. The snooker table was converted into the woodwork table!

The Project leader explained why this approach to reparation had been adopted at North City. The scheme enabled young people indirectly to help the community. Thus profits from the sale of goods had been donated to the local victims' support scheme. There were practical advantages to locating reparation work at the Project – the young people were fully supervised and all concerned were covered by the Project's insurance scheme. The Project leader suggested that alternative approaches to reparation were neither appropriate nor feasible. It was rare for the young people concerned to have committed offences against the person. There was, then, generally no victim to whom reparation might be directed. Methods of restitution to a victim would be explored if it were relevant. There had been instances, for example, where young people attending the cautioning scheme had written letters of apology to their victims. Further, the Project leader referred to her past experience of the significant, practical difficulties in arranging and supervising repara- tion schemes in the community. Ensuring that the beneficiaries are offered a reliable and good quality service poses problems. A final barrier was the difficulty of obtaining insurance cover should persons be injured or property damaged.

The other session at the Project during the week was the Thursday evening session for those who had received police cautions. As many cautions (13) were dealt with in the early months of 1989 as in the whole of the previous year. Project staff had responded to this increase in work by devising a more formal, post-cautioning programme. This programme, completed for the first time during the study, used exercises designed to provoke thought and discussion about offending:

- the first session examined the relative severity of different offences;
- the second session was based on an exercise to explore why those present had committed their offences;
- the third session looked at how wrong it is to commit a range of common offences;
- the fourth, and final, session in the series was a factual exercise about the provisions of the Police and Criminal Evidence Act.

These, then, were the Project's programmes. Who were the main recipients of these programmes during the study?

One week's attendance – a snapshot picture

What follows is a snapshot of the circumstances of the 12 young people who were the main 'clients' of the Project during one week of the study. On the books of the Project that particular week were four young people with supervised activity requirements, five with intermediate treatment requirements to complete, one on a bail support programme and two on after-care programmes. Ten of the 12 were aged 16 or 17 at the time of the study.

Supervised activity requirements

Of the four young people on supervised activity orders, one was attending the Project regularly and cooperating fully with the programme. The second was attending the Project more reluctantly. On a number of occasions he came to the Project with his dog and accompanied by a friend. Contrary to their normal practice staff were permitting this, to help establish a routine of attendance. The third young person had been remanded to care in an Observation and Assessment centre, following further offending. He was still attending North City from time to time, having expressed a desire to complete his order before he reappeared in court. There were, though, difficulties over his attendance related, at least in part, to where he was living. It was not always possible for North City Project staff to transport him to their Project, and staff of the Observation and Assessment centre were not always willing to sanction this young man travelling independently to North City. The fourth young person was failing to attend the Project.

Intermediate treatment requirements

Of the five young people with intermediate requirements, four had
60 days' intermediate treatment programmes to complete, and one a
30 day requirement. They were at various stages in completing their
orders. One had been unable to cope with the evening sessions and
was seen individually, during the daytime.

Bail support

The tenth young person was following a bail support programme.
The provisions of the Bail Act 1976 allow conditions to be imposed
on the granting of bail. One such condition is that the offender,

'...makes himself available for the purposes of...a report to be made to assist
the court in dealing with him for the offence.' (HMSO, 1976)

As the Project leader explained, the appropriate conditions of the
Bail Act were fulfilled if a young person reported to the Project and
cooperated sufficiently for staff to prepare a report. Attendance at
evening sessions could not be enforced, though it might be that the
agreement of a young person to attend a full-scale bail support
programme had influenced the court in favour of granting bail. The
aims of the North City's bail support programme were presented to
the court in the following terms:

'i) to provide a sufficiently intensive level of supervision and control to
assure the bench that the risk of further offending whilst on bail is
minimised.
ii) to ensure that the young offender attends court as required.
iii) to provide the young person with an opportunity to prove his willingness
and ability to keep out of trouble, to enhance his chance of securing a non-
custodial sentence at the final hearing.'

If a young person attended the Project's programmes whilst on bail,
this degree of cooperation could be mentioned in the report to the
court as auguring well for the success of a non-custodial sentence. At
the time of the study, the one young person on bail under such
conditions attended the Project frequently.

After-care

Intermediate treatment or supervised activity requirements can only
be made by the juvenile bench as an addition to a supervision order.
It is likely to be the case that a young person will complete the

intermediate treatment or supervised activity requirements before the termination of the supervision order. Young people attending the Project for – to use the Project's expression – 'after-care', were those who, having fulfilled their intermediate treatment or supervised activity clauses, still had to complete their supervision orders. They had elected to do so through continued attendance at the Project. The Project leader explained that she would expect, at minimum, a once-fortnightly attendance from young people in this situation. Both young people on after-care during the study attended far more regularly than that.

The arrangements for after-care demonstrated the open-ended commitment of the Project staff to the young people in their charge. Further evidence of this commitment was the fact that young people who had attended the Project in the past were welcome to revisit the Project. There were several such visitors during the study.

The group as a whole

These 12 young people on supervised activity, intermediate treatment, bail support or after-care, were all male. The majority were 16 or, just, 17 years of age at the time of the study. (Those aged 17 would have been only 16 at the time their court proceedings commenced.)

The offending records of this group showed a high proportion of theft and handling offences and some car related offences. Also, more seriously, some offences against property – burglary and arson – were recorded, and some offences against the person – assaults and wounding. Prior to their current reasons for attending the Project, six of the 12 young people had previously received sentences including intermediate treatment or supervised activity requirements. These offence profiles, when compared with the known offence profiles of all young people in the city, suggested that the North City Project was dealing with young people who were relatively serious and persistent offenders.

Staff perspectives

The overriding commitment of staff at North City to keeping young offenders out of custody has already been explained. More particularly, in discussions with the researcher, the staff group placed greater emphasis on the management of the juvenile justice system to divert young people from custody, than on the development of treatment programmes for young people while they attended the Project.

The broader task of managing the juvenile justice system will be discussed in the following section. A key element, however, was the constant reiteration in a variety of forums, including the courts, of the willingness and ability of the Project staff to offer alternatives to custody to young people appearing before the courts – not excluding those who had committed serious crimes.

But what targets did the staff group set in their work with young people once they arrived at the Project? And how were these targets reflected in week to week practice?

A preliminary staff objective was to ensure that young people attended the Project. Some young people placed on intermediate treatment or supervised activity requirements were, for a variety of reasons associated with their personal, emotional or intellectual development, unable to cope with the evening programmes. In these instances, staff worked, constructively to establish a pattern of attendance that was realistic. Examples around the time of the research included a young man who, after a period of non-attendance and after warnings had been given, began to attend two individual sessions a week for literacy and social skills work. The Project leader found the best time that she could communicate with another young person, who suffered numerous physical, psychological and family problems, was by allowing him to accompany her when she took her dog for a walk. Another option that had been used by the Project was for a volunteer to work individually with a young person.

The Project staff had clear goals in their work with young people. The Project leader's stated objectives were that, by the time they left the Project, young people should:

- have been confronted with their offending, have talked about the circumstances of their offences;
- have learnt strategies for avoiding being involved in further offending; and
- be clear about the consequences of their actions should they re-offend.

The Project leader argued that informal staff communication with young people – over a cup of coffee or a game of snooker – could be just as important and effective as the goals of a formal programme of work. Staff were observed to take opportunities which arose to encourage and reinforce acceptable patterns of behaviour.

Despite the considerable focus upon juvenile justice management, and a corresponding playing down of treatment models, it remained the case that the staff at the Project paid significant attention to ways in which they could improve the programmes which they offered. This was evident during the study.

At one staff meeting, concern was expressed that the offence programme was not being planned out in advance. Staff were tending to agree what would be done a week at a time. To improve programme planning, it was agreed that staff would try to set aside time for the development of materials. One approach, which the Project staff had already developed on some topics, was to organise offending curriculum and social skills materials into modules to be used over several sessions – for example, drink, driving and health issues could be dealt with in one module. A system of recording how well particular sessions went was mooted, so that practice could be improved when the session was repeated. It was noted that some young people were not doing their work properly and that they should be tackled. The Project leader's aim was to seek a balance between, on the one hand, the tendency to be reviewing material to decide what to do that same evening, and, on the other hand, the danger of producing too structured a programme that did not allow any flexibility to respond to more immediate demands.

Staff involvement in the lives of young people beyond the management of the juvenile justice system was evident, too, in an informal arrangement with the social services district that Project staff could, and did, undertake work that the district staff might equally undertake. It has already been mentioned, for example, that some young people completed the terms of their supervision order by attendance at the Project. The wide ranging role of Project staff was further indicated by the assistance they gave to young people with job seeking or the advice they offered on claiming benefits. Another example was the help given to young people who were heroin addicts, or 'smackheads'. Fully aware that they could only act once these young people sought help, Project staff offered whatever assistance they were able. This included taking young people to the doctor, spending significant amounts of time with them individually or arranging their entry to special units for the treatment of drug dependency.

During the study, staff explained what was most important in their work at the Project: – 'not placing that great a priority on treatment ... other things are more important [that is] ... managing the juvenile justice system'.

The conclusion here is that, while staff may have claimed that managing the juvenile justice system was their first priority, they also did a considerable amount of valuable work with young offenders at the Project. In other words, via their monitoring of young people from the district who were at risk of custody, their liaison with the social services district staff and the police, and their court work, Project staff attempted to minimise the involvement young people had with the court system. If young people were sentenced to attend the Project, however, the staff worked to ensure their well-being in whatever ways they were able.

The volunteers' contribution

As shown already, the volunteers had differing degrees of involvement in the work at the Project, different kinds of responsibilities and different skills which they could bring to bear. There were some common threads, nonetheless, in their accounts of their work at North City.

In general, they were clear as to the goals of the Project and about what their particular contribution was:

'Everyone is aware of the policies ... they are very consistently applied across the board.'

'You know where you stand from the beginning, and that helps.'

Furthermore, they felt that they were trusted to take on responsible work and that their contributions were valued

'you do feel part of the team...not just a volunteer.'

'[I feel that I have] made a significant contribution to the work of the project ...as [I] had the trust and support of staff.'

The volunteers felt rewarded by the reactions of the young people at the Project. As they reported

'[I] get a great kick out of it.'

Particularly satisfying was the feeling that a young person would choose a volunteer to talk to about their difficulties, when they had apparently not talked to others

'If [I] can get them to talk to me ... [then I get] ... great satisfaction ... feeling that [I] can be trusted.'

All this is not to suggest that the volunteers experienced no difficulties in their work for the Project. A practical difficulty for those organising the Wednesday night session was identifying places to go, as there were a limited number of possibilities. Attempts had been made to get the young people to work out for themselves what activities they wanted to pursue on Wednesdays. Yet it seems, in practice, that the decision was often a relatively last minute one and made by the volunteers.

The question was raised as to whether the volunteers always worked together effectively in dealing with difficult situations. Certainly, the volunteers valued opportunities to develop co-ordinated strategies for working with young people. Conversations with the researcher took place at a training weekend. It may have been this coincidence which, in part, prompted so many comments about the value of, and need for, training opportunities.

One concern expressed was that the Project could be used inappropriately – as a safe refuge where young people could discuss and boast about new offences, without danger of repercussions. This concern was not verified by the researcher and was somewhat discounted by another view, that the young people at the Project knew that further offending would be reported to the police.

In summary, the main impression gained by the researcher was that the work of the volunteers at the Project had benefits both for the Project and for the volunteers. Their involvement extended the range of work and activities at the Project beyond what the small staff group could offer. The relatively small group of young people at the Project, their common reasons for attendance, and the staff's clear work strategies, all appeared to contribute to the volunteers' feelings of security and confidence about their contribution.

Some consumer views

The accounts given in this section are those offered by the young people at the Project to the researcher. It should not be overlooked, of course, that the young people may have modified their views, in unknown ways, in order to provide responses which might be deemed acceptable.

There was no ambiguity for the young people as to why they attended the Project. They either had a sentence from the courts requiring them to attend, or were in the court process – a possible outcome of which would be compulsory attendance. They knew that they were expected to stop their offending. How they reported their experiences at the Project to the researcher, however, was somewhat more complicated.

There were broad divisions amongst those who attended. For some, the Project was akin to a social club:

'[I] like coming to the Project. Best thing has been getting to know the lads who come.'

'[I want to come], know everyone here... B...and L... and that ... nothing else to do.'

Others described the Project as a reasonable place to spend time if they had nothing better to do. One was mostly happy to come along except

'... sometimes miss things ... mates going out somewhere good and [I] can't go.'

Some came to the Project simply because they had to:

'[I] just do it.'

Whether they came willingly or not, the informal, social aspects of the Project such as the snooker and the activity nights – what a staff member referred to as the 'nice times' – were reported to be most popular. Typically, what one liked best was the:

'Snooker [and the fact that] a lot of the time is free and we can choose what to do.'

The formal sessions were variously described – as a necessary, but difficult and not wholly comprehensible, evil; as boring and irrelevant; or simply as a chore to be done. As one said

'Work's work.'

Most, admitting to finding the work quite difficult, found it easier to describe what work they did rather than what its purpose was. They knew that staff had a reason for asking them to do the work, but claimed that they were uncertain how it might help them. In the words of two young people

[On Mondays and Tuesdays we do] file work, [we fill in] a sheet, saying [the] thing [we] come here for, why [we] do it ... [it's] just to put in the file ...

show them to someone [don't know who], it tries to help us.'

'[The staff] keep you busy ... [on Mondays we] fill in a sheet of paper [about] getting into trouble, whether your mates agree with it ... it is to learn about crime, how not to do it ... it has helped.'

Others, however, were clear as to how the formal sessions had helped them

'[Now I can say to] my mates ... I'm not going out tonight.'

According to what was reported by the young people, the distinction between the work on Mondays, dealing with offences, and on Tuesdays, dealing with social skills, was mostly not recognised. Some exercises, though, were remembered as having a clear, practical value. Interestingly, for those who had been there, the work on drinking and driving, and drinking and health, was perceived in this way.

Except for one, who regretted the loss of his free Saturday morning, the other element of formal work, the reparation session, seems to have been enjoyed by those involved

'[On Saturdays we] do woodwork ... I like it.'

'... the staff get us to do woodwork ... it's a good idea.'

As one budding fund-raiser said

'we make things and sell them for Barnardo's.'

The reparation session was, it seems, regarded straightforwardly as a practical activity, when new skills could be learnt. No mention was made of community service as a reason for undertaking the woodwork.

One way in which several interviewees thought that coming to the Project had helped them to keep out of trouble, was the simple fact that a significant proportion of their free time was spent there! One stated, candidly:

'around this time, [I] would be in town robbing.'

Another said that

'when [I] first came, [I] didn't have time to come here and go robbing ... didn't have the chance.'

One youth suggested, practically, that the Project should be open until 9.30 p.m. and everyone taken home when the Project closed.

This would remove the main opportunity for offending. Problems of competing engagements could, however, be overcome – to the researcher's knowledge, at least one of the above was subsequently charged with further, similar offences. Also, for the staff, the challenge was to help those at the Project to say 'no' to offending, even when the opportunity was available. Without making any presumptions about their current offending, some of the young people apparently had realised that decisions about offending could be made by them:

'IT can't keep lads out of trouble, [they have] minds of their own ... [the staff] can only advise me ... I can go out and [offend] now if I want to.'

'I've not been robbing for months ... 'cause I decided not to ... not worth it ... I decided myself.'

The young people recognised that Project staff had played an important part in keeping them out of custody. That Project staff had attended court with them, and had prepared reports for them, was commented upon with some gratitude:

'if [staff member] had not come [to court] I would have got put away like.'

Finally, the feature of the Project that was valued by most young people spoken to, was the support and interest of the staff. Most wanted to please the staff, even when they did not agree with their methods of working. Thus, one summarised his judgement of the Project

'Talking about it helps ... more than writing it down and doing paperwork ... don't know what they're on about half the time [but I don't say so] as [name of staff member] is sound.'

They appreciated that the Project is a welcoming place:

'We all get on in here.'

Liaison with other agencies – the juvenile justice system

Young people were referred to the main programmes at the Project by the sentences of the courts and magistrates based their sentencing decisions on the information which they had available to them. Some of that information was supplied in reports written by district social workers. The contents of the social enquiry reports for young people living in the district, and what recommendations were to be made to the courts, were the main subjects of discussion at the fortnightly, juvenile panel meetings held at the Project and attended by social services district staff and North City staff.

The juvenile panel had eight members with decision making rights – seven social workers and the North City Project leader. The panel was chaired by the deputy social services district manager, with the Project leader as the deputy chair. The principal tasks of the panel were:

- to consider all social enquiry report recommendations;
- to offer an arena where district social workers could discuss their work with young people, especially those at risk of remand in care; and,
- to provide a forum for six-monthly reviews of all supervision orders as from January 1989.

A quorum was obtained when three panel members were present. Apart from the members of the panel, social workers responsible for a case attended panel meetings and had a vote in decisions about that case.

The policy of Liverpool social services department was that custodial sentences should not be recommended in social enquiry reports. As far as the North City Project leader was concerned, her role at the Panel was to ensure that the recommendations regarding sentencing also accorded with the tariff system. Use of all non-custodial disposals in the delinquent career of a young offender would delay and/or prevent the use of custodial sentences. Should a custodial sentence be passed by the courts, an 'inquest system' required the panel to reconvene to examine

'i. why the SER recommendation was not accepted;
ii. identification of factors that were significant in the court's decision making;
iii. identification of strategies that could have been adopted to have obtained a successful outcome;
iv. whether or not there was an appeal, and if not, why not.'

The exercise of keeping recommendations 'down tariff' could, for the Project leader, demand a rehearsal and re-rehearsal of the justice or systems management approach. The process of monitoring social enquiry report recommendations was not always straightforward. To draw on examples in the study, if a young person had already failed to complete a community-based sentence at the Project, and there was a strong likelihood of continued non-compliance, the Project leader might be reluctant to recommend another intermediate treatment or, especially, a supervised activity requirement. One reason for this reluctance was the more severe sanctions made available to the courts by the Criminal Justice Act 1988 for dealing with non-compliance. Thus, if a young person was taken back to the court for failing to fulfil the requirements of a supervised activity order, the court would be able to pass any sentence – including detention in a Young Offender's Institution for a period of up to six months. The dilemma facing the members of the juvenile panel, however, when the offences involved were serious, was that it might not seem realistic to make lower tariff recommendations to the court.

The discussions of the juvenile panel could also be complex when a young person had committed a series of offences, of which only some were being considered at his next court appearance. Thus, in one instance, where a young person had several offences outstanding, had previously cooperated with his social worker over a supervision order but not with the Project over an intermediate treatment requirement, the recommendation with regard to the first set of offences was a conditional discharge. This left available the option of recommending an attendance centre order at the next court appearance.

The researcher spoke to seven members of the juvenile panel, including the district manager. The latter strongly supported the work of the North City Project. His active involvement and support of the Project had been evident from the outset. He had sought, precisely, to establish an intermediate treatment centre, with a pure, 'justice' orientation, which would be the focus of all juvenile justice work in the district. He had helped in the recruitment of Project staff; participated in early discussions about policy and practice at the Project; provided office accommodation to the Project staff for the first year; was a member of the Project's executive committee and had formal progress meetings four times a year with the Project leader. Further, the district manager commented favourably on the professional standard of work undertaken by the Project staff in, for example, preparing plans of work with young people for the courts. More generally, the manager supported the involvement of Barnardo's as voluntary sector providers in a mixed economy of welfare in the district. The genuine sharing of responsibility between the district and the Project was demonstrated by the Project leader's role as deputy chair to the juvenile panel.

The six district social workers echoed their district manager in identifying the benefits of the panel system. The panel was described as enabling social workers to make consistent and realistic recommendations to the courts in social enquiry reports. These reports were thought to have improved, professionally, in both their preparation and presentation. North City Project staff's knowledge of the juvenile justice system was deemed a valuable resource for the panel members and the panel a useful training ground for new social work staff. The generally fruitful relationships between Project and district staff were stressed.

None of the social work staff spoken to wanted the panel system superseded and all spoke in favour of the full use of non-custodial options. Their professional and organisational loyalties led them, nonetheless, to question some aspects of the panel system.

On the whole the social work staff were less committed to a rigid application of the tariff system than they perceived the Project staff to be. Thus, first, the stress on justice rather than welfare issues was not wholly accepted. It was suggested that it remained relevant to include reference to the family circumstances of young people in social enquiry reports. Secondly, there was a concern to fulfil one of the major tasks of social workers – to assist, advise and befriend those on supervision orders. It was not thought appropriate that only those who had reached a certain stage of the tariff became formally eligible for this assistance, when it might be needed just as much by those lower on the tariff. Thirdly, it was argued that young people were familiar with the tariff system and might gamble that their next offence would still not receive a custodial sentence. The social enquiry report recommendation, it was argued, should reflect the offence, as well as the stage reached in the tariff. Too close an adherence to the tariff might – taken to extremes – mean overlooking the nature of the offence, its effect on the local community and, even, what was most appropriate for the young person.

While none of those spoken to had observed the evening programmes run at the Project, social workers expressed confidence in the integrity of Project staff and their ability to work constructively with young people. What was mentioned was the wish that the Project would organise separate programmes for girls and younger age groups. This focus on 'preventive' work appeared again to reflect the welfare approach of social work staff.

To conclude, it was clear that district staff had confidence in the work of Project staff with young people. It was also evident that social workers continued to place importance on their welfare role in dealing with young offenders and, hence, differed to some extent with the Project staff group's focus on justice issues.

The cautioning scheme

The cautioning scheme was outside the main programmes of the Project and finances were not allocated specifically for it. The specific objectives of the scheme, to divert young people from the court process, fitted logically, nonetheless, into the Project's overall objectives. The cautioning panel was chaired by the North City Project leader. Members who attended were:

- the police juvenile liaison officers bringing cases to the panel;
- the deputy manager of the social services district;
- a member of the social services district intake team;
- a senior education welfare officer.

The procedure followed was for the cases being considered to be introduced by the relevant juvenile liaison officer, who would have made a home visit. A representative of North City would then report on the home visit they too would have made to the young person and his family. The intake social worker would report what knowledge, if any, the social services district had about the family and, similarly, the Education Welfare Officer would comment on any difficulties at school or over school attendance. Finally, the panel would agree a recommendation for the juvenile liaison officer to make to his superintendent. If the police superintendent agreed with the recommendation, and the recommendation included some intermediate treatment involvement, the young person would attend the Project once the police caution had been administered.

In the period January to mid April 1989, the offences of 13 young people were discussed at the cautioning panel. Of these, 12 were recommended for caution with additional intermediate treatment involvement, one was recommended for a caution only. All 13 recommendations were agreed subsequently by the police superintendent concerned.

The nature of the follow-up intermediate treatment varied insofar as Project staff tried to tailor their follow-up work to the circumstances and offending behaviour of the young person. Thus the structured 'post caution' programme already described was not necessarily used. Other recommendations made by the cautioning panel were that one young person should be encouraged to join a local youth club; and that another should be counselled to deter possible involvement in drug abuse. Issues about which members of the cautioning panel from outside the Project made comments to the researcher were:

- the work of the cautioning panel;
- its follow-up at the Project;
- the target groups with which they would like the Project staff to work.

It was quite clear that the cautioning panel was thought to operate professionally and efficiently. The sharing of information amongst the agencies involved was thought to be useful for possible future contacts with the same families. There was generally confidence in the Project staff's follow-up strategies. As one panel member said

'[the staff] find a way in to talk to the kid, understand his interests and point of view. [They are] then able also to confront [them] with the offence.'

Some points related to the running of the panel were, nonetheless, thought to be worthy of further consideration and debate. For example, it was the police who decided which young people's cases should be brought to the panel. The categories they identified as suitable for consideration by the panel were:

- relatively serious first offenders;
- those who had previously received an unconditional caution;
- some who had already received a caution and attended the Project from one police area only;
- offenders with a court record whose current offence was minor.

All the young people would have admitted that they were guilty of the offence.

The cases before the panel therefore, had, been subjected to a police filtering process. Despite this, some members of the panel felt that some cases considered could appropriately be referred to the courts and that the panel would gain further credibility, in their own eyes and those of the police, were it to be known to recommend prosecution in such cases. Such a recommendation would, of course, have run counter to the purpose of the panel to keep young people out of the court process and, subsequently, out of custody.

Advantages of the panel adopting more formal administrative procedures were also discussed. Examples given included the preparation of a written record, prepared by Project staff, of the panel's discussions and decisions. Another suggestion was for a system for reporting back on the follow-up work that had been undertaken by Project staff. At the time of the study, panel members would not necessarily be informed about this.

The cautioning scheme covered the 10–17 years age range. It was noted that the sNorth City staff had most experience in dealing with persistent offenders, and mainly those towards the top end of the age range. It was thought that the small Project premises and the work experiences and interests of Project staff, could mean that they were less used to dealing with the younger children who might be referred through the cautioning scheme.

The particular expertise of Project staff in dealing with serious offenders was, then, recognised. Yet members of the cautioning panel would also have welcomed a broadening of the Centre's work, to include preventive work with girls and with younger offenders who cannot be brought before the courts.

What emerged from the discussions was some divergence in views between Project staff and other panel members about what were the appropriate roles of the cautioning panel and of the Project. The objective of the Project staff was always to minimise, as far as practicable, the involvement of outside agencies in the lives of young people – especially to avoid their appearing in the courts. The Project staff worked at the cautioning panel to secure an outcome of a caution, or a caution plus some Project involvement. Project staff expressed reluctance to extend further the records kept on young people considered by the cautioning panel, as this would have represented a further intrusion into the lives of these young people. Furthermore, when the panel had been established, the Project staff had explained that they did not have sufficient staff resources to service the panel in this way.

The Project staff's desire to minimise official and unnecessary intervention in the lives of young people, on the grounds that its positive effects remained unproven, explained why the Project did not propose to work with girls and younger children, below the age of criminal responsibility, on what are often termed preventive programmes. Such preventive work was criticised also by Project staff on the grounds of 'net-widening'. In other words, the attention of law enforcement agencies was likely to be drawn to young people involved in such programmes, even if they had not embarked on a delinquent career.

Working at the boundaries

The main, and visible, clients or customers of the North City Project were the young people. This chapter has discussed some ways that the Project collaborated with other agencies, particularly the social services district office and the juvenile liaison officers of the police, to seek and obtain its customers. The other body the Project relied upon for 'custom' was the juvenile bench. Once the bench had made a disposal including an intermediate treatment or supervised activity requirement, responsibility for overseeing that requirement was handed over to the Project staff.

Project staff had, then, to work with two main groups, each of which was likely to exert different demands and expectations. In order to ensure that young people completed the requirements of their various orders, staff had to develop working relationships with the young people. At the same time, the Project staff had to maintain the confidence of the official bodies they served – which varied in their objectives and operational philosophies. Project staff, therefore, were a 'bridge' between the young people and the agencies of law enforcement and welfare. Did this bridging role pose any practical or ethical dilemmas for staff at the Project? An issue which the researcher discussed with the Project leader was how reoffending and/or drug abuse were dealt with. A particular reason for raising this issue was that if staff do return young people to the police for either of these reasons, there was a risk of the young person ultimately receiving a custodial sentence, on grounds of not cooperating whilst on a community sentence. Such a possibility ran against all the stated objectives of the Project staff.

As far as re-offending was concerned, the Project leader explained that it was the agreed and unequivocal Project policy that if young people were known to have re-offended, the police would be informed. If, for example, a group of young people arrived at the centre one evening in a stolen car, they would be reported to the police forthwith. In practice, however, no examples were given to the researcher of Project staff actually having to take such a step. The Project leader suggested that, as her staff would not collude with re-offending, young people would not admit or discuss any new offences with them. The situation that staff faced, she said, was of hearing reports from other young people of offences that one of their peer group was said to have committed. Project staff did not feel it appropriate to act upon hearsay of this kind. Such reports were found often to be exaggerated or to involve the scapegoating of one young person for offences which others had committed.

A similar approach was adopted by Project staff in respect to drug abuse. Some of the young people at the Project, for example those who had been involved in thefts and burglaries, were found to be drug abusers. Their involvement in crime had often been a means of financing their addiction. Staff might have learnt of their drug abuse from other young people or when those concerned arrived at the Project 'smacked-up'. Staff were confident about how to handle and help young people on drugs. In accordance with the law, their policies included the firm rule that drugs should not be brought onto the premises. And formal procedures had been agreed with the police as to how drugs found on the premises would be disposed of. Again, as young people knew the Project rules about drugs, staff argued that it was unlikely that they would ever find drugs on the premises. At the same time, staff could not – and would not – search young people to find if drugs were actually being brought onto the premises.

These two examples illustrate the thin line that Project staff trod. They were realistic about the culture and life-styles of the young people with whom they worked. At the same time, they had to confront young people with illegal behaviour and try not to abet lawbreaking, either wittingly or unwittingly.

Conclusion

The North City Project was well established in offering non-custodial alternatives to young offenders, including persistent and serious offenders. All aspects of work at the Project appeared to pursue that objective coherently and consistently.

A major concern of Project staff was to minimise unnecessary intervention in the lives of young people who had infringed the law.

This task was undertaken by strategies for managing the juvenile justice system – for example, by ensuring that strict and consistent criteria were applied in making recommendations about sentencing, in such a way that non-custodial options were available to as many young people as possible.

The Project dealt essentially with young people convicted of offending or who had admitted their guilt. But they also worked with a few who had appeared in court and were on bail support programmes, but who had not admitted guilt. The Project leader argued against offering preventive programmes on various grounds:

- that it was not possible to predict which young people would become involved in offending;
- that attending a preventive programme might draw young people to the closer attention of law and welfare agencies;
- that the involvement of these official agencies was not proven to benefit young people and might have damaging effects.

The Project's success in achieving its aims could be measured, in part, by the numbers of young people required by the courts to attend the Project's programmes. The 1988 figures quoted earlier in this chapter suggested that young people from North City received the highest proportion of non-custodial sentences including intermediate treatment requirements in the city. Another measure of success was the general confidence expressed in the Project's programmes by the staff of the agencies with which the Project staff worked.

Most of the young people who came to the Project during the study stated their relief at avoiding a custodial sentence. They acknowledged the role of the Project staff in their receiving a community-based alternative and stated (at least to the researcher) their willingness to attend the Project and the benefits they had gained from this.

As one would expect, it was not the case that all young people who came to the Project completed their order or ceased offending. Of the 16 sentenced to attend the Project in 1988, four did not complete their orders. Of the 12 young people included in the study, six had had previous intermediate treatment or supervised activity requirements. The impression gained during the study, nevertheless, was that securing the attendance and cooperation of the majority of the young people was not a significant problem at North City. As noted earlier in the chapter, only one young man failed consistently to attend the Project during the study. He was, after the study ended, returned to court. The others, whilst occasionally absent from evening sessions, were observed to be making progress through their orders.

6. Boughton Hall, Chester

The North City Project, described in the preceding chapter, offered a highly focused service to known and convicted offenders. The overall programme of work at Boughton Hall, to be discussed in this chapter, was broader than at North City, as this Chester project offered alternatives to care as well as to custody.

Aims and objectives

The aims and objectives of Boughton Hall were set out in the Barnardo's North-West Divisional Plan for 1989-93. They were as follows

'... Boughton Hall offers a service to young people aged 11-17 years, living within the Chester District. The project aims to support those who are in difficulty in order to prevent them being removed from their home community...

The *primary aim* of the project is to reduce the numbers of children who receive custodial sentences or who are made the subject of care orders as a result of their delinquency.

The *secondary aim* of the project is to reduce the numbers of children of secondary school age who are removed from home for reasons other than their criminality.'

The statement of aims and objectives went on to outline a complex programme of activities. As far as juvenile justice work was concerned, intervention was said to be of three kinds:

- to prevent young people from becoming involved in delinquency;
- to play a gatekeeping role to minimise the degree of involvement young people who had committed offences had with the court process;

- to provide programmes for convicted offenders which were direct alternatives to custody.

The alternative to care work also had several strands. These were to work with both Social Services and Education staff to prevent admission to care for reasons associated with a young person's welfare or schooling, and, should a young person enter care, to work to minimise the amount of time they spent in care away from home. This chapter elaborates how the Project's formal objectives were actually translated into practice.

The building

The Project was located in a large house set in three acres of grounds, in a suburb about two miles east of the city centre. The Project accommodation, on the ground floor of the house, included:

- two offices for the Project leader, Project workers and secretaries;
- a large kitchen and dining room;
- two main meeting rooms;
- a games room;
- an education room;
- an art room;
- a gym;
- a workshop;
- a computer room.

These were the rooms most in use but there were other rooms not designated for particular activities. There were also outside stores and a motor workshop. The Project building, then, provided almost unlimited space.

The area served by the Project

Boughton Hall offered a service to the City of Chester and its outlying areas. The population of Chester in 1987 was estimated to be 116,900 (Cheshire County Council, 1988). The City has the reputation of being a prosperous tourist centre. At the time of the last household census in 1981, nearly two-thirds of the households in the City were in owner-occupation (63 per cent); nearly a fifth of households (19 per cent) had the use of two or more cars; and over a fifth of the population (21 per cent) was in professional or managerial occupations (Household Census, 1981). The City is, however, by no means uniformly affluent. For example, the estimated unemployment rate for the City in July 1989 was 7.6 per cent. But this rate varied in different City wards, ranging from more than 14 per cent to less than three per cent. (Cheshire County Council, 1989)

While Boughton Hall served the entire City, it was evident that the home addresses of many young people who attended the Project were clustered in two housing areas – Blacon and the Lache estate. Blacon is a distinct community on the north-west of the city. The estimated population in 1987 of the three city wards in which Blacon is situated was 18,440. These wards extend somewhat beyond the geographic boundaries of Blacon and include an area certainly more prosperous than the council-owned part of Blacon. The 1981 Census results for these wards, while providing a slightly better picture than actually existed in Blacon itself, suggested that the area was notably less affluent than the remainder of the City. Thus, over half of the residents (53 per cent) lived in council or new town housing, and very nearly half of the households (49 per cent) were without the use of a car. The unemployment rate in July 1989 was estimated to be around 12 per cent.

The Lache estate is nearer the City centre. In 1984, the estate had a population of 4,320 and had been identified by the County Council as an 'area of family stress'. (Cheshire County Council, 1983 and 1985) County council studies show that in 1981, 25 per cent of the economically active population on the estate was unemployed, 53 per cent of the school age population was in receipt of free school meals, and the number of children in care was twice the county's rate. Data for 1983 shows 60 per cent of the property on the estate to be rented from the council and 60 per cent of households to have no available car. These data clearly indicate the economic and social disadvantages experienced by residents of the Lache estate relative to the population of Chester as a whole.

Juvenile justice in Cheshire

Boughton Hall opened in 1983, around the time that government policies towards juveniles in trouble were reflecting an increased emphasis on diverting young people from the court process, expanding community alternatives and limiting the use of care and custody. In 1983 and 1984, Cheshire developed its own local policies to ensure that juvenile offenders could be dealt with in the community. (Social Information Systems, n.d.)

In order to monitor the effectiveness of its new policies, Cheshire initially used the statistical package and services of Social Information Systems. Subsequently, Cheshire local authority staff took responsibility for the statistical monitoring. Some results from the monitoring exercise are given in Tables 6.1 and 6.2. In interpreting the figures, it is relevant to bear in mind that demographic changes have included a fall in the total numbers of young people in the relevant age group.

Between 1984 and 1988, the monitoring system shows, county-wide, an overall reduction in the number and proportion of offenders entering care and custody. A slight overall increase is also noted in the proportion receiving sentences that were alternatives to care and custody – that is sentences including an intermediate treatment or supervised activity condition or a community service order. In light of county policy, the single most encouraging trend shown by the figures was the marked drop in direct entrants to the courts.

Table 6.1 Sentencing of juveniles in Cheshire: 1984-8

	1984		*1986*		*1988*	
Numbers entering in court	1,595		901		920	
Numbers sentenced to care and custody	126	(8%)	61	(7%)	62	(7%)
Numbers receiving alternatives to care and custody	137	(9%)	104	(12%)	92	(10%)
Numbers of direct entrants*	428	(27%)	190	(21%)	114	(12%)

Sources: Social Information Systems Ltd, Juvenile Justice in Cheshire 1984-86: A Review. Cheshire County Council and Social Information Systems Reports for 1988.
*Direct entrants are those with no previous cautions or convictions.

A review of juvenile justice policy in Cheshire undertaken jointly in 1987 by the Directors of Social Services and Education, the Chief Probation Officer and the Chief Constable, confirmed the main planks of the County's juvenile justice policy. In particular, the review document highlighted the importance of inter-agency collaboration between the Social Services Department and the Police, and adherence to the principles of the 1985 Home Office cautioning guidelines, in reducing the numbers of juveniles appearing in court.

Certainly the significant decline in the numbers of young people appearing in court who had had no previous convictions or cautions suggested improved 'gatekeeping' practices. For those appearing in court, the joint review endorsed the shift to offence-related social enquiry reports and noted an increase in the proportion of SER recommendations implemented by the courts. (Cheshire Social Services Committee, 1987)

In summary, in the 1980s Cheshire Social Services Department adopted a 'systems-oriented' approach to the management of juvenile justice. What were the numbers of juveniles entering the system in the Chester area, that is the area served by Boughton Hall? (*see* Table 6.2)

Table 6.2 Juvenile Justice in Chester: 1984-8

	1984		*1986*		*1988*	
Numbers sentenced	192		103		78	
Numbers sentenced to care and custody	19	(10%)	10	(10%)	8	(10%)
Numbers receiving alternatives to care and custody	20	(10%)	14	(14%)	11	(14%)
Numbers of direct entrants	56	(29%)	19	(18%)	10	(13%)

Sources: SIS publications as for Table 6.1, and locally held data.

Chester City also experienced a considerable decrease, of 60 per cent, in the numbers of young people entering court between 1984 and 1988. The numbers of those sentenced to care and custody also dropped, though the proportions remained stable at ten per cent. The proportion receiving alternatives to care and custody steadily increased – from ten per cent in 1984 to 14 per cent in 1988. In Chester, as in the county overall, the most marked change was the decrease in the numbers and proportions of direct entrants to the court system – from 29 per cent in 1984 down to 13 per cent in 1988.

These figures serve to illustrate the size of the juvenile justice system in Chester. We will now look a little more closely at the sentences which were alternatives to care and custody. Eight such sentences were made in the first six months of 1989 and of these, five included intermediate treatment conditions. In three of these cases, the most serious offence being sentenced for was the taking of a car without the consent of the owner; in the other two cases, the most serious offence was burglary. The remaining three sentences were community service orders – given in two instances where burglary was the most serious offence and in one instance for an unspecified offence.

Project staff

The staffing complement for Boughton Hall was:

- one Project leader;
- two Project workers;
- a part-time volunteer coordinator (25 hours a week);
- a part-time workshop supervisor (20 hours a week);
- part-time secretarial and cleaning staff;
- a caretaker/handyman (working on the general maintenance of the building).

In addition to the normal staffing, over the summer period, a temporary coordinator was recruited to organise the summer holiday activity programme.

The background and qualifications of the professional Project staff who participated in the study were as follows. The Project leader, appointed in 1983 and responsible for the opening and establishing of the intermediate treatment centre, was a qualified social worker with prior experience of intermediate treatment gained in post at Barnardo's Speke centre in Liverpool.

One Project worker, in post since April 1988, obtained her professional qualification and initial experience as a Child Care Officer. She had extensive experience in education as a home tutor and through her work at a special educational needs centre in the city. The second Project worker had recently completed his youth and community work training, and had work experience in youth-work and in sessional intermediate treatment work. The volunteer coordinator began this employment in the Spring of 1988. Her professional qualification was in education. The workshop supervisor had started work at Boughton Hall in August 1987. He had previously worked in the motor industry and was a qualified motor mechanic.

The volunteers

The volunteer coordinator recruited and supervised volunteers to assist with various aspects of the Project's programmes. The notional size of the volunteer group was 20, though the number of volunteers active at any one time fluctuated.

The main volunteer function was to help in the running of an evening activity group. Volunteers also acted as befrienders for individual youngsters with particular needs; assisted in the running of the summer holiday activity programme; and helped young people fulfilling court orders at Boughton Hall to develop constructive leisure pursuits.

The work of the Project: strands of service provision

In 1985, two years after the Project had opened its doors, the Project leader wrote an appraisal document which spelled out the theoretical basis for the project's work with young offenders (Atkinson, 1985). The alternative-to-custody programmes offered by the Project were based, in part, on an understanding of delinquency as 'situational' that is, the belief that some situations were more likely than others to elicit criminal behaviour. The task for the Project staff was

'to help the individual to understand how and why he gets into trouble, evaluate his behaviour in terms of the consequences for himself and for others, and to identify strategies for avoiding getting into trouble in future'.

In other words, the approach was informed by the University of Lancaster's programme of work on juvenile justice (*see*, for example, Denman, n.d.).

The appraisal paper, however, also emphasised ideas from the sociology of deviancy about 'bonding' and 'drift'. In brief, delinquency was thought to follow a weakening of bonds with the established social order. Adolescents who were under-achieving at school and/or unable to enter the job market were particularly vulnerable. This explanation has been supported by data on offending which show a drop in delinquency rates in early adult life. The practical strategy advocated to combat delinquency was that Project staff would try and foster the links and bonds which young people had with their community and their families. Thus, transgressors would be subject to greater normative controls and would have more to lose if apprehended.

The final argument in the appraisal paper was that a lesson to be learned from youthwork practice was the value of offering young people opportunities to partake in new, rewarding activities and to experience 'good, caring adult models'.

The focus in this thoughtful appraisal paper was firmly on theory and models of practice for dealing with young offenders, as befitted the primary objectives of the Project. At the same time, the appraisal acknowledged that a more broadly based clientele was likely – and needed – to ensure adequate use of the Project's resources. For example, the Project had developed an activity-based programme to provide a

'compensatory and diversionary experience for children with a wide range of problems. Broadening the referral base… in this way is one of the main purposes of the activities programme. Social workers are able to consider referring children other than the severely delinquent…'.

It was clear that young people attending the activity programmes would be referred by social workers, but specific criteria for such referrals were not given in the appraisal – particularly as far as girls were concerned.

A year later, in September 1986, a review undertaken by County advisers (Jarret and Cormick, 1986) reiterated the different client groups at Boughton Hall as, first and foremost, serious and persistent young offenders; but also

'Children who have been identified as being in danger of getting drawn into anti-social behaviour…

Children who are lacking social skills and opportunities for achievement and who are therefore at risk of offending…

A day care group requiring a more intensive support, including help with education.'

The authors of the review paper commented on the small numbers of persistent offenders at risk of receiving custodial sentences and, hence, potential clients of the Project. They recommended that an appropriate extension of the justice work would be for the Project to develop community alternatives to remand to care, and to develop reparation and mediation services.

The review paper authors also noted that Barnardo's and Chester District were committed to a 'welfare' model for dealing with young offenders and were exploring how the 'welfare' and 'justice' models could be coordinated. This seems to imply that Project staff were trying to ensure both that the welfare needs of the child would be addressed and that any intervention would be limited to the just deserts of punishment.

A third issue raised in the review concerned the combination of work undertaken at Boughton Hall. It was suggested that running 'activity' programmes at Boughton Hall could undermine the Project's credibility with magistrates, and also lead to young people being inappropriately labelled as potential offenders. It was argued that a more appropriate strategy would be to run youthwork programmes in the localities where the young people on the activity programmes were actually living.

To sum up, the Project was intended to work, above all, with young offenders but there was always an openness towards undertaking preventive or care-related work with other young people referred by social workers. Further, there are some pointers that staff thinking about objectives and methods of work was more fully developed with regard to the main priority group, young offenders, than with other referral groups. Finally, in some quarters at least, concerns were expressed about the wisdom of linking too closely alternative-to-custody and alternative-to-care programmes. These issues are pertinent to an understanding of who attended Boughton Hall, and why.

Table 6.3 Attendance at Boughton Hall during 1988

Main reason for contact	Male	Female	Total	(%)
Juvenile justice work				
Intermediate treatment	7	1	8	(12)
Supervised activity order	2	–	2	(3)
Pre-court work (with those	4	1	5	(8)
who did not attend otherwise)				
Supported cautions	2	–	2	(3)
Intensive 'alternative-to-care' work				
Alternative-to-care	7	3	10	(15)
Less intensive 'alternative-to care' work				
Wednesday night group	9	3	12	(18)
Summer holiday programme	14	4	18	(28)
Other				
'After-care'	2	–	2	(3)
Project assistants	1	1	2	(3)
Befriending	3	1	4	(6)
Total	51	14	65	(100)

Workload

A detailed breakdown of workload prepared by the Project leader for the calendar year 1988 shows that staff worked with 65 young people during the year (*see* Table 6.3).

What these figures suggest is that just over a quarter, 26 per cent, of the young people came to the Project for reasons associated with their offending – that is, prior to a court appearance, to fulfil a community-based sentence, or as part of a supported caution. Fifteen per cent attended for relatively intensive alternative-to-care work, and 46 per cent were offered activity group programmes designed to prevent likelihood of admission to care. Thus, in total, 61 per cent attended for some form of 'care' related work. Of the remainder, three per cent were Project assistants – the term that is explained below, six per cent came for befriending programmes and three per cent came for what was termed after-care.

Available information suggests that Boughton Hall offered a service mainly to adolescent males. Just over half of the young people attending in 1988 were 15 or 16 years of age. All of those sentenced to attend the Project to fulfil intermediate treatment and supervised activity conditions were 15 or 16-years-old.

Of the 65 young people at Boughton Hall in 1988, 19 had had prior involvement of a different kind. This raises the question, often asked by critics of intermediate treatment, as to whether young people on preventive programmes were being brought prematurely to the attention of law enforcement agencies. These figures, albeit limited to one year's work, do not suggest 'net-widening'. None of the young people on intermediate treatment or supervised activity conditions were recorded as previously attending an alternative-to-care programme, the Wednesday night activity group, or the summer holiday programme.

Young people and their careers at the Project

The two principal referral routes to Boughton Hall were the courts, for young people serving a community-based sentence, and the social services department, for young people being offered a programme designed to reduce the likelihood of entry to care. The true picture of who attended Boughton Hall, why, and what they did when they were there, was rather complicated. For example, some young people entered care and still attended Boughton Hall; others fulfilled the requirements of their court order and still chose to continue to attend the Project. These varied careers will be illustrated here by discussing two fictitious but (hopefully) plausible case histories.

Two invented case histories, exemplifying possible careers through Boughton Hall

1. Henry Henry first got into trouble for shoplifting when he was 12. That time he was cautioned. He managed to stay out of further trouble (or out of police sight) until he was nearly 14. Then he was caught shoplifting again. This time the local police agreed with their social work colleague that Henry needed more attention than he would receive from a straight caution. It was decided to offer a caution on condition that Henry attended Boughton Hall for several sessions. Henry duly attended Boughton Hall on four occasions after school, when he met the Project leader and did some work on why and when he offended, how to avoid these situations, and how to say 'no' to his friends.

The sobering effects of the the caution were not long-lasting. Three months later, Henry was arrested on burglary charges. This time he appeared in court and received a sentence of conditional discharge. Six months later, he appeared in court again, also on burglary charges, and received an attendance centre order. He did not comply with the order and, when he was arrested for theft from a motor-vehicle, he again appeared in court. Before he was sentenced this time, he spent a little more time at Boughton Hall. This was to determine whether Henry would cooperate with a community-based sentence. Henry remembered the pool room and seeing people in the grounds riding motorbikes and readily promised his cooperation. His parents were only too anxious to support any measure that would keep Henry out of trouble – and out of custody. The Project leader spoke in court on Henry's behalf, confident that Henry would complete an intermediate treatment condition. Henry duly received a one year's supervision order with 30 days intermediate treatment condition. This was the first of two orders Henry was to undertake at Boughton Hall, the second a supervised activity order. Henry told his mates that Boughton Hall was great – particularly the bikes. In fact, Henry was not always happy about giving up his free time twice a week after school. Nor was he keen, as he phrased it, on 'sitting in a room and talking about his offending – why he did it... you talk about some things, and then have to talk about them again!' At Boughton Hall, Henry heard that he would probably grow out of offending. Before he did, though, he was charged for several more burglaries and for taking and driving away a car without the owner's consent.

At 15½ years of age, Henry received his first custodial sentence. When he finished the sentence, he was virtually of school-leaving age. His second day of freedom, he dropped into Boughton Hall, was welcomed by the staff and invited to stay for a meal. The Project staff talked to him at length about YTS placements and arranged that, while he was awaiting a placement, he could spend one day a week at Boughton Hall as a Project assistant, doing some jobs in the house and grounds, for which he would receive some expenses.

Henry turned up for a week or two and then got onto a YTS scheme. He continued to return to Boughton Hall when dissatisfied with the scheme. The staff maintained their friendly interest in him but hoped that he would finally move on from their ministrations, which, in due course, he did.

2. *Eddie* Eddie's social worker contacted the Project to see if the staff could offer any help. The social worker knew Eddie's family quite well. Mrs. George had found it difficult to cope, financially and emotionally, after the break-up of her first marriage. She had been at her wits end trying to control 14-year-old Eddie and, had it not been for the social worker's support and intervention, Eddie might well have ended up in care. The new worry was that Eddie had started staying away from school. He had been placed in the special unit as he was bullying other children and disrupting classes. Eddie resented being in the unit. Initially, the social worker asked if Eddie could join the Wednesday activity group – his energies would be safely channelled one evening a week and he would receive some additional attention and care from his volunteer linkworker and from the volunteer coordinator. Fortunately, there was a place in the group that could be offered to Eddie, that of a girl who had not attended for some weeks.

Eddie enjoyed the Wednesday group sessions and participated in all the activities. However, although he told his mother that the group 'takes the steam out of me', he continued to miss school. The school contacted the social worker and a planning meeting took place between Eddie and his mother, the social worker, school and Boughton Hall staff. It was agreed that Eddie would attend Boughton Hall two half-days each week, on afternoons when he had lessons at school which he found particularly irksome and where it was unrealistic to expect him to make progress. He was to do constructive activities at Boughton Hall, cookery and bike sessions, and work to gain the Project's own certificates indicating certain standards of achievement. It was hoped that this package would avert court proceedings for non-school attendance.

Eddie responded well to the care, interest and stimulation he received at Boughton Hall. He was never absent from his sessions. His attendance at school, though, remained erratic. It transpired that he had a job. He had taken the job to earn money, which his mother could ill-afford to spare him. But the part-time delivery work meant that he missed some school. Eddie felt frustrated that he should not be allowed to work to earn money and was expected to spend his day at school – for him a time-wasting and unprofitable occupation.

In his final year at school, the social worker, the school deputy head and the Boughton Hall Project worker to whom Eddie had been allocated, agreed yet another package. Eddie would spend two days a week at Boughton Hall and three at school. At Boughton Hall he would spend some time in the mornings doing formal school work on subjects and topics he would not be covering in school. In the afternoons he would continue with his various activities but would also be expected to contribute something to the household economy – by helping to prepare lunch, cleaning the minibus and so on.

This package lasted pretty well during the first term of the school year, with constant checks taking place between the school and the Project that Eddie was where he was supposed to be, and with some overlooking of a reasonable number of absences from school. Matters deteriorated at home, though, and Eddie entered voluntary care at the Children's Centre. He continued his joint programme at Boughton Hall and school. When Eddie officially left school, he also left the Children's Centre for what, optimistically, was planned to be 'independent living'. Not unexpectedly at his age, he found the combination of trying to live and cope on his own and his YTS placement, hard to sustain and he relied heavily on the support of Boughton Hall staff. For a while, he undertook part of his YTS placement at the Project by special arrangement. It was a little while before the staff finally said goodbye to Eddie.

These adapted case histories illustrate two possible careers through Boughton Hall. Not all young people had the degree of involvement indicated above. For some, involvement began and ended with Wednesday activity group membership or with attendance at a summer holiday activity programme. If young people were attending school or were in employment, they might complete their intermediate treatment or supervised activity conditions simply through a series of evening attendances and have no further contact with the Project. The point is that Boughton Hall offered packages and programmes for *individuals* – the hallmark of the Project was its flexibility of approach.

Completing an order at the Project

In accordance with the Project's practice of developing packages for individuals, there were no 'standard' Project programmes for intermediate treatment conditions or supervised activity orders. There were, however, certain core components in the packages devised. The goal was to ensure that, wherever possible, young people fulfilled the requirements of their order. In outline, the packages divided into five main areas of work:

- *Offence-focused work* Work on the order began with individual discussions with young people about their offending, using interactive computer programmes to chart the situation and context of the offending. Next, some groupwork on offending was generally undertaken including exercises on attitudes to victims, legal rights, and what was – or was not – gained from offending.
- *Social skills* Some social skills work was tackled, sometimes in group sessions, and included work on temper control, coping with school or help with independent living skills.
- *Reparation* The reparation work undertaken by young people at Boughton rHall was to help the workshop supervisor run the regular, weekly sessions, when adults and children with physical and mental disabilities rode the specially-adapted, all-terrain-vehicles in the grounds at Boughton Hall.

    Establishing worthwhile reparation schemes for young offenders is difficult – programmes involving service in the community can be hard both to establish and to supervise effectively. Further, projects working with only a small number of offenders can find it difficult to sustain a community service, such as gardening for old people, which recipients may have come to rely upon. The Boughton Hall scheme, organised 'on site', reduced problems of management and supervision to a minimum. The problem of continuity of service was overcome by the workshop supervisor running sessions with the assistance of young people attending care-related, as well alternative-to-custody programmes.
- *Constructive leisure pursuits* Some constructive leisure pursuits were introduced, these included riding the motor-bikes at Boughton Hall (of which more below) or going swimming, skating, canoeing or hill-walking.

● Counselling Finally, some counselling on welfare issues was offered by Boughton Hall staff, focusing on individual difficulties being experienced by young people at home, school or work.

Three characteristics of the intermediate treatment and supervised activity order programmes were evident. First, the timetable for attendance was adapted to individual circumstances. Those who were attending school or were in employment attended after their working day. Others, some of whom were in care placements and neither attending school nor at work, attended during the day.

Secondly, the supervised activity order and intermediate treatment programmes were very similar. For example, the reparation work with the bikes had been intended only for those completing supervised activity orders. However, in practice it was undertaken also by those fulfilling intermediate treatment conditions. What was important to the Project leader was that the intermediate treatment condition offered another, pre-custody step on the tariff ladder.

The third feature of these Project programmes was that they could lead to the award of Project certificates for completion of certain, set tasks. Thus, the workshop organiser in post during most of the study had worked out a three-fold programme for work with the motor bikes. The three units of work focused on correct riding skills, a knowledge of relevant law governing the use of motor vehicles on the road, and motor bike maintenance. The purpose of the package was to offer young people at the Project the legal opportunity to undertake something which, through offences of taking and driving away, they were often involved in illegally. It was also felt to be important that they learnt the appropriate skills which would lead to safety on the roads once they were legally entitled to drive.

This system of unit accreditation for completing specified tasks was one adopted in other activities at the Project – in woodwork, in preparing meals, in music and so on. The tasks required were relatively straightforward and planned to be well within the capacity of the young people for whom they were designed. Their value was in structuring and rewarding the development of basic skills in young people involved, who often had no recorded achievements whatsoever.

The researcher certainly received positive feedback from young people and their parents about this strategy. For example, at a mothers' group meeting, Ron's mother said how pleased Ron had been about getting a Project certificate for picture framing 'He now has a horrible poster in his room(!)' Another young person showed the researcher with some pride his three framed certificates, hung in the corridor at Boughton Hall.

The alternative-to-care programme

There were four strands to the alternative-to-care programme:

- intensive alternative-to-care work;
- less intensive alternative-to-care work;
- the summer holiday activity programme;
- the project assistant role.

Intensive alternative-to-care work

This programme catered for those defined as being at severe risk of entering the care of the local authority. Frequently, these young people were having difficulties at school. Boughton Hall staff had close links with several city secondary schools and with the city's special education needs provision (though the Education Department had not contributed to the funding of the Project).

The package that Boughton Hall had developed with the schools, and were offering to several young people during the study, was one whereby the young people attended their school for part of the week and the Project for the remainder. The relative amounts of time spent at each place depended on such factors as the level of difficulties experienced at school and the possibility of the young person returning, full-time, to mainstream schooling – the young people concerned were generally placed in special units in the schools.

While at Boughton Hall, the young people followed a programme which included some formal schoolwork, some social skills activities, some free time for using the computer and some opportunities for riding the motorbikes. Apart from the substitution of schoolwork for offence-related work, in fact, the days of those on this alternative-to-care programme were not dissimilar to those of young people on intermediate treatment or supervised activity orders.

Less intensive alternative-to-care work

Less intensive alternative-to-care work was undertaken throughout the year through the Wednesday night activity group. This was run by the volunteer coordinator and staffed by her and a group of volunteers. Referrals to the group were made by social workers and the main criteria for membership were family stress or behaviour problems which could, ultimately, lead to entry to local authority care. Some of the members had, indeed, been admitted to care and continued to attend. Members at the time of the study had experienced, variously, repeated admissions to care, having problems at school, or were thought to be on the fringes of offending.

The group was held between 5 and 7 p.m. and the routine was to spend three evenings at the Project and to devote the fourth to an outing. At the Project, the group was run rather along the lines of a very structured youth club. There was some free-time early in the evening, for playing pool and table tennis or for chatting. This was followed by a planned activity – arts and craft, cooking, a treasure hunt – then time for clearing up and relaxing. Each activity group member was linked with a volunteer and the last ten minutes of the evening was set aside for the volunteer link person to talk to his or her two group members. The volunteers were then expected to complete a short log sheet for these young people, on any issues arising. On the fourth week, outings in the minibus included ice-skating, swimming, ten-pin bowling and once, with consequent numerous bruisings, an eventful trip to the dry ski-slope.

The summer holiday activity programme

A second activity oriented programme was the summer holiday programme. This programme was designed

'to alleviate family stress over the summer holiday period;
to reduce the likelihood of admission to care;
to reduce opportunities for offending;
to provide an experience of working in groups alongside good adult role models.' (Atkinson, 1989)

To achieve these aims, the Project ran a four-weekly programme. In 1989, 33 young people, referred by social workers or Boughton Hall staff, attended the programme. The particular reasons for referral were left to the judgement of social workers.

During the programme, the young people who attended were offered four activity sessions a week. These included canoeing, biking, football, way finding (including treasure hunts and orienteering) cookery, arts and crafts, and drama. There was a 77 per cent attendance rate of young people on the programme. One young person was admitted to care during that time and one was known to have offended.

The Project assistant role

The final element in the alternative-to-care programme concerns the opportunities offered to those who had attended the Project on any of the programmes described, and who had no settled employment and little support in their lives. Young people in these circumstances were offered the chance to act as Project assistants, to undertake part of their YTS placement at the Project, or, simply, to drop in and talk to staff and share a meal or have a cup of coffee. During the study, half a dozen young men came to the Project regularly, and several others intermittently, seeking additional personal support and interest from the Project staff. These young people were often struggling to cope with living on their own for the first time, having recently left care or custody.

The Project assistants were, by definition, older than other young people at the Project, the eldest of the occasional attenders being 18-years-old. The Project staff endeavoured to timetable and structure the participation of these young people at the Project, assigning tasks and routines. At the same time, however inconvenient and inopportune the demands made, staff were virtually always supportive and welcoming. At the extreme, during the study this involved having to deal with two (exceptional) incidents of aggression and one of theft.

The weekly routine

How did these various activities dovetail into the weekly programme at the Project? During the study, Monday mornings were kept as free as possible for staff meetings, but there was sometimes a group or individual session in the afternoon. The bulk of work with young people was undertaken between Tuesdays and Thursdays. Each of these days was divided into four sessions. Before 11 a.m., there was time for staff planning, recording, individual visits, or other meetings and administration. Around 11 a.m young people started to arrive. From 11–12.45 p.m. approximately, was the first work session. This could be an 'education', 'offending', or reparation session undertaken with individuals or groups. Between 12.45 and 1.45 was lunch-time, then the early afternoon was spent on particular activities or outings. The early evening session, from 3.30 p.m.

onwards, was for any young people attending school or work, but also required to attend the Project. On Wednesdays, the activity group convened around 5 p.m. On Friday mornings there was sometimes a work session but, in general, this was a day for winding up the affairs of the week. There were reparation sessions, on alternative Saturday mornings.

On top of this notional, weekly timetable were court attendances and meetings of various interest groups. Project assistants might attend any day of the week and require supervision. Frequently, there were only a few young people in the building, but their supervision was relatively intensive.

Particular plans for each week were agreed at the Monday morning staff meetings – and who would be responsible for doing what, with which young people, was recorded on a planning board in the office.

A fixed point in any day when young people were in the building was lunch-time. Lunch at Boughton Hall served as a training ground, a sociable forum and a workplace – in addition, of course, to its nutritional function. A two-course, cooked meal was generally prepared. Young people working for a cookery unit might help cook the meal. Certainly all young people at the Project were expected to help with the meal in some way, either by preparing the food, laying the table or washing-up. These were not popular tasks but were normally done, after some persistent reminders by staff. While not forgetting the groans and outbursts that could take place from young people, lunch at the Project was nearly always a pleasant occasion and one in which everyone, whether or not they were eating the prepared meal, participated.

Staff perspectives

Thee first staff priority was the alternative-to-custody programme and related offending work. The numbers on this programme were fewer than on the alternative-to-care programme; however, as the Project leader pointed out, the time and effort devoted to those on the alternative-to-custody programme was generally greater.

As we have seen, the alternative-to-custody programme was underpinned by a particular analysis of young people's reasons for, and circumstances of, offending, and the Project's programmes were designed to intervene accordingly. The researcher identified no comparable analysis to underpin the second main focus of the

Project's work – the intensive alternative-to-care programmes. Such an analysis might have examined the reasons why, and circumstances in which, young people came into care and how the Project's programmes should address these issues – and thus help to avert entry to care. The early documents about the Project's work suggested, rather, an intention to establish criteria for acceptance onto the alternative-to-care programme through experience and practice.

Project staff commented favourably on the flexibility that this more pragmatic approach had allowed them. Nevertheless, the desirability of focusing the alternative-to-care programme carefully was also acknowledged by them. In practice, young people at the Project were most often thought to be at risk for behavioural reasons. They were beyond the control of their parent figure, and/or were not attending school – though it is perhaps worth noting here, that the Children Act 1989 removes truancy as a precursor to care.

At the end of the research study, the Project leader began to frame some tighter criteria for acceptance onto the intensive alternative-to-care programme. For example, he suggested that the programme was relevant to young people who had large amounts of free-time as they were not attending school; young people who were on the fringes of care and for whom Boughton Hall could provide somewhere to belong. The overall objectives of Boughton Hall were to continue to be to prevent admission to care and programmes would be designed to enable the young person to 'engage in purposeful activities designed to foster a sense of achievement and self-worth, to develop social skills and appropriate behaviour sufficient to survive in the real world'. (Atkinson, 1989)

The prime aim of the model of practice adopted by Project staff towards those on the alternative-to-care programme was to strengthen and develop links which the young person had with his or her local community, on the grounds that this would reduce likelihood of entry to care. This could involve Project staff working with schools, local youth organisations and potential employing agencies – as well, of course, as with the young people concerned.

An important element in the alternative-to-care programmes was the possibility of offering a young person a combined package of attendance at Boughton Hall and their school. Such packages were agreed with individual schools and relied, largely, on the goodwill and cooperation of relevant staff in the school. The precise agreement reached was, then, linked to what staff at individual schools felt was appropriate. During the study, one school made its cooperation dependent on the young person concerned reliably attending school at the agreed times. As the young person failed consistently to cooperate in attending school, the Project staff were unable to allow him to attend Boughton Hall during the day. This was unsatisfactory precisely because it left the young person with a great deal of idle time. Experience suggested that some other schools would have adopted a more flexible approach – if only to ensure that the young person was under adult supervision for at least part of the school week.

A significant issue here, it seems, was that the Education Department did not have a formal link with the Project. Home-tutors had used Boughton Hall as a base in the past but there was no funding from the Education Department for the liaison work Project staff undertook with schools, nor for the educational input and general supervision offered to some young people during school hours. It had not proved possible to reach a more satisfactory agreement with the Education Department, though this had certainly been attempted.

Whatever the reasons for a young person's attendance at Boughton Hall, for the outside observer, a key component of the Project's strategy was to provide consistent, caring support. Caring attitudes and actions were sustained through all the normal vicissitudes of a centre dealing with troubled adolescents – that is, when young people were unresponsive; when they failed to appear for agreed sessions or turned up when they had promised to attend school or go to work; when they cooperated only reluctantly with a planned session; when they lacked concentration and dropped-out from agreed tasks or activities before they were complete; when they were verbally aggressive; and so on. The staff made their disapprobation of such behaviour clear but also demonstrated their continuing commitment and forbearance.

The development of the Project assistant's role demonstrated this fundamental concern for young people. During the study, a group of young men came into the Project, one or more times most weeks, who had begun, or were about to begin, living away from either the Children's Centre or the family home and who were seeking or trying to settle into employment. The Project leader felt that they relied heavily on the support the Project offered and that it should continue. To extend and formalise this help, Project staff planned an independent living group programme, which was implemented after the study ended.

The volunteers' contribution

The main point made by volunteers was their satisfaction that they could offer the young people at the Project their friendship and, in return, would occasionally be shown that their interest and commitment was appreciated. Thus one valued:

'the feeling of being friends with kids that are deprived of friendship; the kids are very rowdy but you get out what you put in.'

Another remembered the time when the boy for whom he was keyworker defended him strongly from the criticism of another group member. A third felt that:

'far too many want to put young people down [but they need to] feel valued as they are impressionable.'

Managing a group by firm but sensitive means, and by offering good 'role-models', did not necessarily come naturally to all the volunteers, particularly when they first began volunteering. One, particularly, remarked on the temptation simply to control and discipline. However, whatever the tasks they were expected to perform or the style in which they were to perform them, the volunteers generally agreed that they received appropriate support from the Boughton Hall staff. Particularly welcomed were the training sessions arranged by the volunteer coordinator.

By and large, the volunteers felt that their role was a significant one in the eyes of the young people. They suggested that the young people appreciated that the volunteers gave up their own time, unpaid, to help run groups. They felt also that the relationship between the young people and volunteers differed in kind from the more professional relationship which existed between staff and young people.

The possibility of attending planning meetings with social work and school staff was referred to gratefully. The significance was that a young person would know that his volunteer would be present to offer support at important, and perhaps less pleasant, times as well as during the more enjoyable occasions at the Project.

In conclusion, the volunteers spoken to seemed satisfied with their role at the Project. Some were fitting their volunteering into busy lives and felt unhappy that they could not offer as much help – or as reliably – as they would have liked. It is part and parcel of any volunteer coordinator's role, however, to cope with a transitory volunteer population. Certainly during the study, there was a core of dependable volunteers who extended the range of provision that the Project could make to both day and evening attenders.

Some consumer views

The voices of some young people have been heard already in the case studies. Those to whom the researcher spoke did not have uniform experience of the Project – they had attended the Project for varying lengths of time, for different reasons and had followed individual programmes. What is reported here simply offers a 'flavour' of their reactions to Boughton Hall.

An important preoccupation of the young people fulfilling non-custodial sentences was with the proportion of their sentence which they had completed. While maintaining a detached stance towards the work they had done at the Project encouraging them to reflect on their previous offending, they had apparently – consciously or unconsciously – learnt one of the main lessons:

'It's up to you if you want to stop. Nobody can make you – you have to make up your own mind.'

'No-one knows yourself better than yourself...[the staff] can talk till they're blue in the face...only you know whether you've decided not to offend.'

There was some appreciation of the intentions of the staff in structuring their time at Boughton Hall. As one said:

'[The Project leader] sets rules and doesn't give way. Can't cross him...can't go too far...[I] broke it a few times like...but still respect it.'

But, there was also some feeling that it was possible to opt in and out of the programme:

'You do what you want here...it's a waste of time...It is really for younger kids...who are not so set in their ways.'

This young man felt that he would be more likely to be deterred from offending by having to compensate a victim 'the full whack'.

The favourite activity was the bike project. Even the most cynical enjoyed riding the bikes and were prepared to do the required reparation work to gain a ride. Several also enjoyed other leisure pursuits, while appreciating their purpose:

'[the activities] keep you out of trouble...stop you being bored...get to do things you wouldn't otherwise do.'

Those on the alternative-to-care programme also enjoyed the activity sessions and generally enjoyed coming to Boughton Hall:

'better than hanging about the streets'

and, as another altruistically said:

'it gives my Mum some peace and keeps me out of trouble.'

The education work was also accepted – partly because the time devoted to it was relatively short! But one young person also felt that he understood the schoolwork that he did at the Project more, because he received more help and explanation than at school.

So, the researcher encountered some cynicism and bravado amongst the Project's adolescent consumers. But the overall tenor of the comments was, at least, accepting – and, at best, very approving.

Finally we look at some parental perspectives. The mothers the researcher spoke to were those who attended a parents' group, established and run by one of the Project staff. The group offered some mutual support and companionship for the mothers of some of the boys on the alternative-to-care programme. These mothers were quite confident that their sons enjoyed coming to the Project:

'They are buzzing when they come home.'

The Project provided opportunities and activities for their sons that these mothers could not, for they were mostly bringing up their children on their own, in difficult circumstances.

Amongst those whose sons were attending Boughton Hall as part of a school/Project joint package, there was confidence that their sons came to Boughton Hall, though less certainty as to whether they attended school regularly. There was some regret that one or two, who attended school with the greatest reluctance and only under some considerable pressure, could not attend Boughton Hall every schoolday.

The mothers were very appreciative of the help, support and interest displayed in their welfare, and that of their sons, by the Project staff. They said that coming to the evening meetings at the Project kept them in touch with the experiences of their children.

Liaison with other agencies: the juvenile justice system

The organisational links which Boughton Hall had with the juvenile justice system were with:

- the Police;
- the juvenile bench;
- the Social Services Department's Court Officer;
- other social work staff who prepared social enquiry reports and who maintained regular contact with the Project, via a series of review or planning meetings, during the time a court order was being completed.

The Social Services Department's Court Officer was the key link person in the Chester juvenile justice system, as far as Boughton Hall staff were concerned. It was he who met the Police Community Department's sergeant each week to receive information about all enquiries to the police involving juveniles. The Court Officer also then discussed the police cautioning recommendations. At this meeting, possible referrals to Boughton Hall for post-caution sessions were agreed, as were any referrals to the activity programmes. The meeting served in lieu of a cautioning panel with a wider membership. At one time the Project leader had attended the police liaison meetings, but the practice had been discontinued. It is worth recording that Chester had a high cautioning rate, the highest in the county of Cheshire in the first six months of 1989 – 89 per cent.

Some supported caution work was undertaken at the Project during the research study. The work focused on the offending behaviour and included exercises on reasons for offending, being in trouble and on self-control. This approach was reported to be standard practice at the Project. The representatives of the police branch to whom the researcher spoke seemed content with the liaison arrangements. They pointed out that they received feedback from the Project leader regarding the post-caution work. The Court Officer also played an important role in the format and presentation of social enquiry reports to the courts. There was no juvenile panel to screen social enquiry report recommendations in Chester – the Court Officer coordinated that function. If the case was unallocated, the Court Officer prepared the social enquiry report himself. As far as allocated cases were concerned, the social worker wrote the social enquiry report. At the time of the study, social workers in Chester were working generically and any social worker could be required to prepare a report. The Court Officer's task was to assist them. His advice would be based on the tariff system, trying to keep young people in the community for as long as possible. If a young person was well known to the Social Services Department and was beginning to move up the tariff, then a more formal consultation process would take place between the social work staff, the Project staff, the young person and his or her family. The Court Officer would normally present the social enquiry report in court, though the social worker might be present also.

If the report's recommendations suggested a non-custodial sentence, then a member of the Project staff would be in court, having prepared a report describing the precise programme to be offered and the likely response of the young person. The researcher's observation was that Project staff worked hard to gain the cooperation of young people who were appearing in court, and to design and agree appropriate programmes for them.

Sometimes a social enquiry report would recommend a relatively low tariff sentence and, as a means of obtaining the bench's agreement to the recommended option, the possibility of Boughton Hall staff undertaking some additional work was offered. During the study, an example of this was when three girls quite seriously assaulted a fourth girl. The victim's family decided to press charges. The court sentenced the three girls to pay compensation. It was further agreed in court, though no order was made, that the girls would attend six follow-up sessions at Boughton Hall. The three girls were remorseful about their actions and one aim of the follow-up work was to effect a reconciliation between them and their victim. This was successfully achieved as far as two of the girls were concerned.

A separate strand of collaboration was some preliminary work undertaken jointly by the Court Officer, Project leader and head of the Children's Centre to try to develop alternative packages for the courts so as to prevent young people from being remanded into care. Boughton Hall's involvement was to be in providing bail support packages. This, mutually valued initiative, had not been finalised at the time of the research study.

Various viewpoints were expressed in discussions with the researcher about the juvenile justice system operating in Chester. Two issues are raised here. First, it was clear that the general principles adhered to by Boughton Hall staff were those in the justice model – a model which advocates a proportionality between offence and punishment. Thus, when four first offenders received custodial sentences, staff from the relevant agencies were consulted urgently. It was the case, however, that such inquest activity was informal, as indeed were the consultations between social workers and the Court Officer and/or the Project leader when social enquiry reports were being prepared. In discussions, social workers pointed out that even when they consulted the Court Officer, they were not bound by his advice. On the other hand, a number of the social workers spoken to clearly valued the knowledge and advice available via such consultations and agreed that it was in their interest to use the consultation system if custody was a possible outcome.

The Project leader suggested that, though the system was informal, the results suggested that it worked well. He appreciated that 'gatekeeping' could be more formally and tightly managed – and he would have preferred *automatic* consultations over social enquiry reports, to facilitate full and accurate monitoring of the juvenile justice system.

If the informal system of gatekeeping worked well, it was perhaps because those involved were keen to implement their shared objectives, and because they were fairly confident in having a satisfactory degree of support from the local juvenile bench. Certainly, a prominent member of this bench stressed to the researcher his eagerness to avoid giving custodial sentences. What this representative of the bench did find a matter of concern was the amount of re-offending, indicated in the follow-up reports which the bench received from Boughton Hall.

The value of a more formal 'gatekeeping' mechanism – a juvenile panel system, for example – is that it does not rely as heavily upon individual goodwill for its conscientious implementation.

The second issue was the occasional practice of offering to undertake additional work at Boughton Hall with those being sentenced, to make a low tariff sentence more acceptable to the bench. The Project leader was well aware of the risks in this strategy. For example, the bench might feel that they should formalise the offered work and make a supervision order with an intermediate treatment condition – in other words, a higher tariff sentence than that recommended in the social enquiry report. Alternatively, if the Project did undertake some informal work, on a subsequent appearance in court, the young person involved might be thought to have already experienced the equivalent of an intermediate treatment requirement and receive an even higher tariff sentence. In practice, therefore, careful consideration was given as to whether, and how, reference to such informal work would be made in any court report.

Care-related programmes and collaborative working

The important links on the alternative-to-care programme were:

- with the social workers who were the referral agents;
- with the schools where young people were pupils;
- with Appleton House, the local Children's Centre, if the young person was in care.

Care planning

Social workers wishing to make a referral to Boughton Hall generally had a preliminary discussion with a staff member about the young person's circumstances and immediate problems. If both parties agreed that the Project could offer a relevant service to the·young person, the second stage in the referral process was a formal request from the social worker to Boughton Hall. At this point, Project staff completed their own referral form, including information about the young person, their family and current difficulties.

The main liaison mechanism was the 'care planning meeting' which took place at the outset, and at intervals throughout, a young person's placement at Boughton Hall. These meetings were similar in format to those which took place to review progress on alternative-to-custody programmes. Always invited to the meetings were the young person and a member of his or her family, though they did not invariably attend. Also present were a member of Boughton Hall staff and the social worker in charge of the case – school and Appleton House staff were represented where relevant.

What kinds of issues were of common concern to those present? On one occasion, it was the reluctance of a former Project assistant, who was living at the Children's Centre, to continue his YTS placement. He had considerable personal difficulties and was finding his work placement difficult. He had been in trouble with the police in earlier years and seemed on the fringes of offending again. He was not abiding by the rules at the Children's Centre, which he had outgrown. In contrast to the concerns he was posing for the Children's Centre, at the Project he generally behaved responsibly and helpfully – the Project staff agreed to offer him continuing support during this difficult patch.

Another care planning meeting attended by the researcher took place in a local secondary school and focused on the behaviour, at school and at the Project, of a young person whose twice weekly attendance at the Project was designed to provide him with some additional support and attention during an unhappy time in his family life. The young person concerned valued the greater freedom of the Project and the opportunity to undertake pursuits normally unavailable to him. He did, however, also cooperate with the less exciting aspects of the Project, such as the chores. In conjunction with his attendance at the Project, the school had also made arrangements which gave him greater support in school.

The evidence presented at this planning meeting was that the young person was attending school more regularly, his behaviour in class was calmer and his bullying behaviour towards other pupils was occasional rather than routine. One thorny issue raised by the school was, given his liking for attending the Project, how to avoid it seeming to this pupil that his bad behaviour in school was rewarded by time at the Project. Another dilemma, raised in this and other discussions with schools, was how to ensure that a pupil did not reduce his chances of academic achievement by spending time out of school. This primarily concerned younger, more able – albeit disruptive – pupils.

Links with the Social Services Department

The social work managers associated longest with the Project, confirmed that the reason the Project expanded into alternative-to-care work was the comparatively small numbers in the juvenile justice system receiving community-based sentences. As one manager explained:

'There was an element of opportunism in the move to family break-up preventive work.'

But it seemed also that, historically, Chester district had had a welfare-oriented, preventive focus in its work with adolescents – those at risk of trouble as well as potential contenders for local authority care. It was, therefore, felt to be a natural extension of the

Project's work to become involved in preventive care work. One manager pondered:

'where do you draw the line and say any area of work is inappropriate, especially when staff are motivated,'

At the same time, he appreciated that while this approach had been accepted as valid, there was now a concern that some observers 'may not feel that activity at Boughton Hall is focused'.

No manager stated any reason for concern about the quality or range of work at Boughton Hall, though the headway made by the 'justice' approach in recent years was referred to. If Boughton Hall fell into the classification of broad-based intermediate treatment centres (Bottoms,1987), what reasons did field social workers give for referring young people there?

One reason described to the researcher was that the Project served as an extension to a relatively hard-pressed fieldwork service. The Project undertook work that fieldworkers said they would have done in the past – that is, devoting significant amounts of time to the care and support of young people in difficulties and helping them develop constructive leisure pursuits. Project staff had, it was argued, the luxury of time to spend with young people, plus the appropriate setting, space and equipment.

Furthermore, it was acknowledged that the Project staff had developed specialist skills for working with young people when family breakdown was likely. Some of the social workers felt that their own skills were strongest in dealing with adults, or, that they did not have the sufficient time and resources to work satisfactorily with both adults and children in a family. There was, therefore, a belief and confidence that Boughton Hall staff excelled at working with young people:

'Boughton Hall is very flexible...offers a quick response to a young person in difficulties...often crucial in preventing family breakdown and they have expertise in dealing with young people.'

It was suggested that Project staff got to know the young people and their family circumstances better than social workers – they got to the root of problems and opened up opportunities for resolving important issues. As as one social worker described the process, it was 'relationship building in a cocooned environment'.

Referrals were also made for school related problems. One respondent argued that such a referral was most relevant when it was endorsed by the courts as a last measure before further court proceedings were initiated. Others welcomed the option of Project intervention at an earlier stage in school attendance problems.

These accounts related to young people referred to the more intensive, alternative-to-care programmes. Some referrals to, for example, the summer holiday activity programme were made simply because the Project could offer comparatively deprived young people opportunities for challenging pursuits. In this capacity Boughton Hall was offering a good youthwork service. Several respondents were critical of the city's own youth provision, particularly in the areas where many of Boughton Hall's customers lived.

The discussions with fieldworkers tended to confirm an absence of, as one manager termed them, 'copper-bottomed referral criteria' and that, as he continued, referrals were based 'on social workers' knowledge of the resource and deflection from care in the broadest terms'. Certainly there seemed to be several models of the Project's role which informed social workers' decisions as to when it was appropriate to make a referral and to which programme.

In her discussions, the researcher also sought reactions on the range of programmes offered at Boughton Hall. One concern expressed by social workers was whether young people on the alternative-to-care and alternative-to custody programmes were always kept separate. Most stated that, while they approved very much of the alternative-to-care packages, they thought long and hard before they made a referral as they did not feel it appropriate, for instance, for school refusers to mix with persistent offenders. They also worried, if a young person who had attended the Project ended up in court for non-school attendance, that there might be assumptions about their having offended. As one said

'I thought very carefully about referring C..., I did not want to put him on the Boughton Hall path.'

The researcher's observations suggested that, normally, members of each programme were timetabled to attend the Project at different times. However, in practice, there was inevitably some overlap between the two groups. On such occasions, work sessions generally continued to be run separately but the two groups were likely to meet at lunch and perhaps during an activity session. It should be stated that there was no direct evidence collected during the research study to suggest that such contact led those on the alternative-to-care programme into offending.

Links with secondary schools

Social workers made referrals to the Project but the cooperation of the schools was important in sustaining some placements. The objectives and tasks of schools differed from those of Boughton Hall and had to be accommodated. It was certainly practicable – one school in particular, which sent several young people to the Project, had established a good working relationship with it.

The researcher spoke to three representatives at the secondary schools with which the Project had most dealings. In summary, the pay-off for the schools in cooperating with the Project was if the young people behaved better in school. The reality was that some pupils settled down in school, while others did not. It was hard to measure precisely what contribution the Project had made when behaviour had improved.

School staff appreciated the involvement they were invited to have in devising individual Project programmes for their pupils and the fact that they were asked to attend care planning meetings. Communication between school and Project was regarded as especially important where it was possible that young people would attempt to play staff groups off against each other. Schools had less involvement with the Project over those pupils who only attended the activity programmes but, again, were grateful that these programmes offered valuable leisure time pursuits and may have diverted some pupils from offending. The schools welcomed the experience some Project staff had had in education. However, there was a significant view held that not all Project staff were interested in how young people behaved in school, even though this behaviour could usefully have been focused upon in Project counselling sessions.

There were two areas where the Project's aims and those of the schools were sometimes out of step. One was the difficulty for school staff in accepting – as they perceived it – that it was disruptive pupils who benefited from the Project. School staff said that they would like many more young people in school to experience the constructive leisure pursuits at the Project.

The second issue was also about selection of those who attended the Project. Schools were happy for those who were 'marking time' at school before they left, to attend the Project. They were less happy to allow younger pupils, who had potential for some academic achievement, to spend time away from school in the day – though such pupils would never spend more than half a day per week at Boughton Hall. School staff also remarked that, as the National Curriculum was implemented, there would be further difficulties in sanctioning time out of school.

The Children's Centre

During the study, communication between the Children's Centre and the Project appeared very good. For instance, a staff member from the Centre was involved in planning the independent living group with a Project worker and it was likely that the group's members would include some residents of the Children's Centre.

The Children's Centre and the schools had in common their continual responsibility for young people who attended Boughton Hall only once or twice a week. Further, both institutions were also responsible for a number of others who did not attend the Project. The practical issue for both schools and Children's Centre was that young people could return from the Project very excited and voluble about their experiences. This could cause resentment amongst other young people and difficulties for supervising staff.

Conclusion

This chapter has described the work of Boughton Hall. In summary, Boughton Hall offered services to young people who were known offenders, to young people who were at risk of entry to local authority care, and to some who had already entered care.

Those convicted of offending were referred to the Project by sentence of the court. All those on the alternative-to-care programme were referred to the Project by social workers – though, if the problem was school-related, the original concern may have been raised by school staff or an education welfare officer. Not all of those young people were at the some degree of risk of entry to care. Generally speaking, those on daytime programmes had more likelihood of entering care than those on the summer and evening activity programmes. A number on each programme were thought to be on the fringes of offending – some had already received police cautions.

Some young people were encouraged to attend the Project once their formal programme had ended. Once they were 16-years-old, if their attendance was comparatively frequent, they might be given the title of 'Project assistant' and asked to spend some of their time working in the house or grounds. A few Project assistants later became volunteers.

There were, naturally, some differences of approach and emphasis in the work of different members of the Boughton Hall staff. The predominant ethos and main characteristics of the Project staff, however, were to help and care for the young people with whom they worked. While staff made clear their disapproval of some behaviour, overall, during the study they were observed to be tolerant of anger and frustration displayed by young people and to seek constructive ways for resolving the practical problems which provoked such behaviour. Social work practitioners commented with particular approval on:

- the ready availability of Project staff for discussions about how best to help young people face their problems;
- their willingness to devise individual programmes;
- their undaunted persistence to 'get through to anyone' and 'to think the best of everybody'.

Social workers in the city tended both to endorse minimising intervention in the lives of young people convicted of offending and, pragmatically, to accept the broad-based programmes of the Project – though most would have preferred those convicted of offending to be dealt with wholly separately.

Young people who were completing, or had completed, non-custodial sentences at the Project stated some boredom and ambivalence towards the offending work that they were required to undertake. They, and those on the alternative-to-care programmes, were far more enthusiastic about other aspects of what the Project had to offer, especially the bike project.

An interesting feature of the Project was the 'reparation' scheme which enabled young people fulfilling court orders to offer a vulnerable section of the community evidently enjoyable new experiences. There was a commitment to offering this service, even when there were no young people fulfilling court orders at the Project.

7. Speke Intermediate Treatment Youth Centre, Liverpool

What distinguished the Speke centre from the other projects included in the study was that, in addition to its alternative-to-custody and care-related programmes, it offered a neighbourhood youth and community service.

Aims and objectives

The specific objectives for the Speke centre as stated in the Barnardo's North-West Divisional Plan in autumn 1988, were:

'The primary aim of this project is to reduce the number of juvenile offenders aged 10-17 years of age living in south Liverpool who are committed to care or custody.'

'A secondary aim of the project is to work with any young person within south Liverpool who is referred to the centre because they are experiencing difficulties with life and the problems of adolescence.'

The relative priority placed on each service which the project offered was elaborated in a report presented to the local authority's social services committee during the fieldwork:

'[In] descending order of priority:
i) Alternatives to custody – three or more sessions a week here (I.T. Orders and Supervised Activity Orders).
ii) Alternatives to Care – one session a week (preventive work).
iii) Youth Club and Activity Groups – a variety of youthwork open to all young people and using a lot of local volunteers.'

A fundamental strand of the Project's stated philosophy was

'The Centre believes that it is essential for their project to avoid becoming associated in the minds of the local community only with delinquents and the Youth Club "label" is vital in this respect' (Colenso,1988).

The particular benefits of the youth and community provision for the young offenders attending the Project were elaborated in the Divisional Plan in the following way:

'By being aware of the dangers of "labelling" young people as deviant, and the consequent risks of confirming delinquent identity, the centre aims to project a positive image to the local community, by providing a wide range of auxiliary activities run by local volunteers for young people from the area, regardless of whether they are referred for delinquent activity or not. Such activities presently embrace drama, canoeing, rugby, sailing, stock car racing, climbing, netball, football and Duke of Edinburgh Award.'

In summary, then, the Project aimed to provide:

- alternatives to custody for young offenders;
- alternatives to care for young people at risk of entry;
- a broader youth and community service, in part to help avoid the negative effects of segregating and labelling offenders.

This mix of justice, care and community work objectives can be traced back to the early days of the Project. For example, when the centre first opened, the planning group thought it important to offer a youth and community service in order to reduce the hostility expressed by residents about the acquisition of the building by Barnardo's and its planned use. With what resources and to what kind of area was the Project offering these services?

The building

The intermediate treatment Project was in a former Salvation Army building. Inside the building there were, downstairs, three staff offices, a small meeting room mainly for the volunteers, an arts and craft room and a large hall/gymnasium; and, upstairs, a small kitchen, open-plan coffee bar and pool area and another meeting room. There were cellars and other storage cupboards for the Project's quite considerable camping and outdoor pursuits equipment and for other Project paraphernalia. There was a garage alongside the centre with access from within the building as well as externally. The current banger for stock car racing, go-karts and other car maintenance and welding equipment were kept in the garage. The Project's minibus and landrover were parked in a commercial garage elsewhere on the estate. The Project's canoes and boats were also stored away from the centre – near the river and marina where they were normally used. The furnishing of the centre was basic but, despite heavy use and some abuse of the building, the interior was kept in good order. For security reasons all rooms, bar the cloakrooms, were kept locked when not in use.

The exterior of the building was mutually acknowledged to be unwelcoming. The upstairs and downstairs windows had wire grills over them, the flat roofs were spiked with metal fencing. The main entrance was in the car park to the rear of the building. This entrance was kept locked or bolted and, as there was no door bell, staff and visitors alike sought entry by hammering on the door with a metal latch. The car park was frequently littered with broken glass and other debris. On a number of occasions during the fieldwork cars were climbed on, kicked and rocked by youths misbehaving in the car park.

The emphasis on security inside and outside the building could be attributed to break-ins and thefts experienced at the Project. These ranged from the dramatic burglary described by one staff member, when the burglars tunnelled through the Project walls so as to avoid triggering the alarm system and equipment of considerable value was removed from the building; to instances of minor, opportunistic theft as when, during the fieldwork, three youths allowed into the Project for a few minutes took the chance of an unlocked office door to take the stamp box and its petty cash.

The area served by the Project

The intermediate treatment Project was in a side street close to the centre of a large council owned estate on the outskirts of Liverpool. The estate was a self-contained community with its own shops and schools. The Project opened in 1980 to provide a service to this estate.

Since then, the area served by the Project has been increased twice. When the research was undertaken, the Project was working with young people from almost the whole of the south of the city, an area containing well over a quarter of the city's population – 138,600 of the city's 491,400 inhabitants (Liverpool Social Services Research Section, 1985 and 1986).

In socio-economic terms, the Project's catchment area had:

- just under a quarter of the city's households of lone parents with children (1,209 or 24 per cent of such households);
- around a fifth of the city's overcrowded households (just over 2,000 or 21 per cent of such households);
- just over a fifth of the city's economically active population who were seeking work;
- just over a fifth of the city's children in care – that is, the children's home addresses were here (around 270 or 21 per cent of children in care);
- nearly a quarter of the city's council housing stock (17,800 council dwellings).

These summary statistics disguised pockets of both extreme deprivation and, in part of the locality, of affluence. They are useful mainly for illustrating the geographic and population size of the Project's catchment area. What they do not effectively convey is the absolute social and economic deprivation found in much of this area – the adverse consequences of which were experienced by most of the young people who came to the Project.

Juvenile justice in south Liverpool

In 1988, approximately 18 per cent of the 749 sentences passed on juveniles in the City related to young people from the Project's catchment area. This area was covered by two social services districts but the sentences passed were not evenly distributed between them. The district in the immediate neighbourhood of the Project served around ten per cent of the city's population, and ten per cent of the number of young people sentenced in the city's courts were from this district. The other social services district, with around 18 per cent of the city's population, produced – on this admittedly limited measure – only seven per cent of the city's juvenile justice work. The Project was, then, located in the district which generated much of its juvenile justice work. However, the numbers of community-based sentences passed on young people from the two districts in 1988 were almost identical. The main sentences passed on young people from the whole catchment area included six intermediate treatment requirements, six supervised activity orders and five community service orders.

Sentencing data for the whole of Liverpool suggested that young people from the two south city districts had a marginally better than average chance of receiving a relatively low tariff sentence. Thus eight in ten (80 per cent) of all main sentences passed on these young people were lower on the tariff than an intermediate treatment requirement – across the city, 76 per cent of all main sentences fell into this category. The proportion of high tariff sentences, to youth custody and detention centres as they then were, was seven per cent in south city – exactly comparable with the proportion in the city as a whole.

Project staff

The Project had a staff group of eight, plus two part-time cleaners. At the time of the study, these staff were:

- one Project leader;
- one deputy Project leader;
- three Project workers, one of whom was in a temporary appointment.

One of the posts was funded with LAC(83) money to help the Project develop its alternative-to-custody programmes. These staff had a mix of childcare, social work, youth and community work qualifications – the temporary project worker, with a background in residential work, did not hold a professional qualification but was applying for a CQSW training place. In addition there were:

- a vehicle instructor who was a qualified garage mechanic;
- a part-time volunteer coordinator;
- a part-time clerk typist.

Collectively, the existing staff group had substantial experience in working with young people, gained in a variety of community, school and residential settings. They also had considerable, relevant expertise, including outdoor pursuits and drama skills, to use in their group work.

The volunteers

In addition to the paid staff, the volunteer coordinator had established a group of about 13 or 14 volunteers who offered assistance of some kind to young people at the Project. For example, volunteers helped at the youth night or ran activity groups, and some drove project vehicles to transport youngsters to and from the Project or elsewhere.

The local Social Services District manager was instrumental in setting up the Speke centre and, at the start, members of his staff worked jointly with the Project staff. By the time of the study, district social work staff were not as closely involved with the running of the Project, but continued to help with the running of some groups. They were not, however, working with any of the groups during the fieldwork.

Workload

The main description of the project's activities will focus on the treatment groups running during the study period. First of all, though, it is interesting to review the workload of the Project over one year.

During the year July 1987 – July 1988, Project staff undertook – or, in a few cases, had recently begun – some sustained work with an estimated 53 young people. Of these, 24 were termed 'heavy end', in other words they were young people either completing non-custodial sentences or being considered for such sentences. Eleven of them had received supervision orders with intermediate treatment requirements, six were subject to supervision orders with supervised activity requirements. One youngster had, at different times, been on both types of orders. Four of the youths had attended the Project as part of a bail support scheme and two had come to the Project prior to their court appearances, to enable staff to assess their suitability for community based sentences.

Eighteen of the 53 young people were girls, mostly aged 14 or 15. Fourteen of these had been referred to the project by social services district staff – the remaining four came to the Project as friends of referred girls. Fifteen of these girls were members of one of the two girls' groups run in the year, which were designed primarily to help girls in, or on the margins of, care. Project staff worked individually with the other three girls.

Another group run during the year was a 'Home on Trial' group for 11, mainly younger, children. These children, boys and girls, had almost all been recently discharged from care and were at different levels of risk of re-entering care generally because of poor school attendance. (As noted elsewhere in this book, the provisions of the Children Act 1989 will preclude truancy serving as grounds for entry into local authority care.)

A great number of the young people attending the Project were living in difficult circumstances. Many were living outside the parental home – with relations, in a foster home or residential establishment, or in other, unstated, circumstances. A high proportion of those of school age were either in an education guidance unit, a special school, or had no school place at all.

In addition to the membership of the groups already described, around 40 young people were on the register of members of the Project's youth club. The club, which ran on Wednesday evenings, offered local young people art and drama, cookery, sewing and sports activities. Some of these youngsters were also members of activity groups run by the Project – the fishing club, the rugby team, the Duke of Edinburgh Award scheme, and so on. The registers for these activities suggested that membership and actual attendance at the activities fluctuated over the year.

As well as the registered workload of the Project, staff had dealings with other young people on a more informal basis. Thus, staff made initial visits to young people who had been referred to the Project but who did not subsequently join a group. Staff also helped the friends of members of groups – one example, which occurred during the fieldwork was when staff negotiated between one such friend and her parents when the girl ran away from home. In addition, during the study, a number of past members of 'heavy end' groups came to the Project and talked to staff or helped in the garage.

What did the group membership numbers and other activities at the Project mean in terms of attendances each week? Over a 14-week period between January and April 1988, the total weekly attendances recorded in the register ranged from 75 to 153 attendances per week. Weekly attendances for this period averaged out at 109 attendances. In every week but one, the highest numbers of attendances were recorded on Wednesday night when the youth club was held.

Most of the young people who used the building were of school age, so the greatest use of the building was in the evening, after school hours. During the day, staff used the office facilities. On some days, members of the motor group worked in the garage, and at lunch-time, some of the girls' group used the coffee bar facilities, and some members of the intermediate treatment group made use of the sports hall and pool table.

The weekly routine

Most youngsters with whom Project staff undertook sustained work were allocated to one of the treatment groups run at the centre. The particular mix of groups running at the Project at any one time depended on the numbers and types of referrals the Project had received, and on the available staff resources. The three groups running during the fieldwork in the late spring and early summer of 1988 do, however, illustrate a range of the Project's work.

This section will discuss who attended these three groups – and why, the groups' staffing, and the programmes of work and activities offered. It will also make some very general comment on the apparent impact of involvement with the Project for members of the groups. This account by no means covers all work undertaken with members of these groups by Project staff; some other aspects of work with the youngsters will be highlighted when the ways that the Project worked with other agencies are described.

The intermediate treatment and supervised activity orders group

Henry   Henry had just reached school leaving age. He had not, however, attended school regularly since being suspended, two years previously, for threatening a female teacher and because of his frequent, severely disruptive, behaviour in the classroom. Following his suspension from school, he was placed in an educational guidance unit. He only attended the unit on three occasions. He appeared in court seven times, on a variety of charges which included theft of a motor vehicle and attempted burglary. He lived with his father. His mother and siblings lived elsewhere in the city. Following arrest for his last offence, he was remanded in custody but later obtained bail, on the understanding that he attended a group at the intermediate treatment Project in Speke. He attended three group meetings in five weeks. Henry's family was well known to the Project, as his older brother had been a member of a 'heavy end' group. This brother later served a prison sentence for armed robbery. His 17-year-old sister occasionally came to the young mums' group at the Project. Henry himself used to attend a younger children's, summer activity group.

Henry is a *fictitious*, but plausible, member of the Project's intermediate treatment and supervised activity order group. One certain characteristic of all members of this intermediate treatment group was that they had been charged with an offence or offences and had either appeared in court and received a non-custodial sentence, or, were due to appear in court and were being considered for such a sentence. Offences committed by members of this group at different times included:

- burglaries;
- attempted burglaries;
- theft;
- attempted theft;
- going equipped for theft;
- handling stolen goods;
- criminal damage;
- assault;
- breach of the peace;
- threatening behaviour;
- unlawful taking of a motor vehicle or being carried in such a vehicle;
- driving whilst disqualified;
- attempted theft of a car.

The intermediate treatment group that was running during the study began in early April, closed to new referrals in May and continued until August. Any members with outstanding time on their orders were then allocated to a member of staff for individual work until the beginning of the next group, or the expiry of their order. In mid April, before the group was closed to new referrals, the researcher discussed its membership with the lead staff member. At this point there were 11 'members' of the group, all at quite different stages in their delinquent and court careers. Five of these members had also been in an earlier group but had not completed the terms of their orders in the life of that group.

Four of the 11 members of the group were fulfilling court orders. A fifth youth was also the subject of a court order but, at an early stage of the group, went into custody following further offending. His continued membership of the group was in doubt. Five of the remaining members were in the court process and awaiting a sentencing decision. Three of these were attending the group as part of a bail support scheme, with a fourth attending the group from a 'care' placement, having offended while on a bail support scheme. This young man could only attend the Project if escorted there by a staff member. During this period, staff were assessing whether it would be appropriate to recommend non-custodial sentences to the courts for these youths. They were not undertaking social work assessments. Rather, the staff were exploring whether the families could support these young people in the community, and looking into the motivation and cooperation of these young people and their parents. The eleventh member of the group, having already completed an intermediate treatment order at another Project, was attending the Project on a voluntary basis. His link with the justice system was that he was subject to a deferred sentence from the court.

Even this snapshot picture illustrates the inherently unstable membership of the group, in large part because of continuing offending. At this early stage two, potential members were, respectively, in custody and remanded to the care of the local authority. And this situation remained typical throughout the life of the group. In May, the project meeting minutes on the group read:

'Heavy End working nicely as a group. Still individual problems with non-attendance. A. a problem. B. is in Risley. C. is on the run. D. is coming. E., F., and G. are turning up ... F. is in court on Tuesday 10th May.'

By early September the project meeting report on the group read

'H. had a warrant issued on 2nd September. I. – wheels are in motion to breach him...J. deceased. (He was run over by a train whilst on the run). C. has not turned up at all. I. is in custody. B. is in court in Thursday and Friday. D. has finished. He is in court on Friday re bike incident. A. – still trying to get him in, maybe to try weights. Still waiting for new social worker. Maybe it needs to be considered taking A. back to the panel. G. attending O.K. I. [staff member] to help with alcohol problem. Court date is soon. F. – in (Observation and Assessment Project) at the moment. Up on robbery and blackmail...'

Membership of the group was, of course, also dependent on decisions made by the courts. For example, E., who had attended the group in its early stages for assessment purposes, was sentenced to four months youth custody when he appeared in court.

The group was staffed by the deputy project leader, the more experienced of the two female project workers, the vehicle instructor/project worker and, during his placement, a student. The advantages of this staffing ratio were acknowledged by staff; several of the staff group had worked together before and knew when best to step in and take over from, or back up, another member of staff. Careful planning and coordination could be important in maintaining control over a disruptive group. An example explained to the researcher was of a staff group agreeing, prior to a residential camp, that if a certain level of disruption was reached, the camp would be disbanded and the lads brought home early – as in this instance, they were. Conversely, when few young people attended the heavy end group this could be too weighty a staff group and, on occasion, a member (or members) of staff would withdraw.

The programme for those in the group fulfilling intermediate treatment requirements, or being considered for recommendation for such a requirement, was the then standard Project programme of two evening sessions a week – one providing an 'offending' curriculum and one intended to foster acceptable leisure pursuits. The general format of the offending curriculum was described as follows:

Offending curriculum

'This session is very much a work session where the nature of each person's offending is examined in detail. Use is made of role-play and other structured exercises to give group members insight into what motivates their actions, and so help them develop strategies for avoiding becoming involved in criminal activities in the future. We also look at the consequences of their actions, for themselves, their families and the victims of crime.'(Report to the court, 1988)

The session offering constructive leisure pursuits was for many of the youths on intermediate treatment orders, particularly those involved in car related offences, the motor project run at the Project:

'The work in the garage is an adjunct to the groupwork which goes on with all the referrals at the centre. Thus, if a lad gets an order made for crimes which include motor crime, he will be asked to attend this group... we now have Stockcar racing in the summer months and Karting, Trials Biking, Bike-ability and Landrover green-laning in the off season.' (Colenso, 1988)

In the motor project the young people were also offered limited training in basic mechanics and welding. They prepared the car for the stockcar racing and some helped in negotiating the initial purchase of the banger.

Two additional weekly sessions in the programme for those on supervision orders with specified activity requirements were a reparation session and an individual counselling session. The reparation session was some form of community service and included, for example, young people working at a residential organisation for children with learning difficulties. Discussions with the member of staff primarily responsible for arranging reparation schemes, and reports at team meetings, indicated that finding, agreeing and supervising suitable and worthwhile placements were time-consuming tasks. A number of organisations could be contacted and negotiations begun before a placement was finally set up. One difficulty noted during the study was that potential host organisations were sometimes – understandably – reluctant to allow young people with convictions for theft and burglary to have access to, and knowledge of the storage arrangements for, expensive office or video equipment.

The counselling sessions focused on how members of the group were progressing with the rest of their programme and on giving practical assistance in helping to find job training placements, trying to obtain employment or helping with social security claims. One youth was helped to join Alcoholics Anonymous for assistance with his drink problem. These sessions are not reported in detail here, but, nonetheless, they are a significant element of the staff's workload.

During the life of an intermediate treatment group there were also some residential periods for all members, which were spent under canvas or in a cottage, when time could be spent on outdoor pursuits and when staff hoped to get to know the members of the group better.

Over the study period, considerable staff energy was devoted to enabling and encouraging members of the group to come to the Project – for example, staff would call and collect members prior to meetings, particularly those who lived at a distance from the Project, and evidently returned frequently to the homes of those who had not come to a group session. However, the degree of cooperation obtained from the group was observed to be highly variable. Some members repeatedly broke appointments to come into the Project, failed to stop offending, and could be uncooperative and unruly at the Project.

One evening group session that the researcher observed illustrated the uphill task that sustaining the interest and cooperation of even a small group could be. A general plan for a groupwork session on offending might be to try and introduce the session in a lighthearted way with a game, followed by a more serious trust and disclosure exercise and to end with another light game or event. This particular group had rebelled against games, and the staff had agreed to try and use more adult approaches – such as focused discussions. (Despite their concern to be treated as adults, however, this particular evening started with one member throwing a stink bomb!)

For the first activity of the evening, the members were asked to select a car or cars from a pile of advertisements and explain their selection to the rest of the group. All the group, bar one member, participated in the exercise with apparent interest if, in one case, with considerable sleepiness. The exception repeated over and over again that he did not want to play silly games. For the second exercise of the evening, a chart of offences committed by the group was put up on the wall. Staff tried to focus discussion on the main offences committed by the group whose members, for their part, showed some interest in 'who' had done 'what'. Some of the group discussed the premises they chose to burgle and why. They argued, diversely, that burglaries should be restricted to cars and shops, or that rich people can afford burglaries as they can reclaim losses on their insurance. With some difficulty, the staff were able to maintain the interest of all but one of the group up to that point. Interest and concentration dropped markedly as the next exercise was introduced. The task for the lads was to list their five most recent offences, whether or not they had been caught offending, and to state who they were with while they were offending. By this stage the lads were lying back with their feet on the table and were asking when they could go home. Some information was obtained with difficulty and the coordinator attempted to draw together the results. The evening ended with a short game of pool and refreshments.

What was unclear as an observer of this session was whether the group members understood the purpose of the exercises they were asked to do. The demands of completing the evening's programme seemed, on this particular occasion, somewhat to overshadow staff efforts to challenge the types of offence being discussed. The staff were aware of the dilemma and later raised the issue as to whether the plans for a session, and its objectives, should be explained more specifically to the group at the start of the evening.

The researcher's impression, confirmed in discussions with other agencies, was that overall the staff of this heavy end group were reluctant to give up working with any member of the group. Staff were prepared to negotiate and re-negotiate, to try and achieve a working relationship with all members of the group and enable them to complete the terms of their order as required by the courts. By the end of the fieldwork, however, staff were preparing the ground for breaching at least one member of this particular group, who had certainly stretched the skills, resources and patience of the staff.

Not all groups or sessions at the Project were as taxing. For example, the researcher also observed some group sessions of a different 'heavy end' group. These sessions made use of video recording techniques. The group was first taught to use the camera. Once the basic skills had been mastered, the staff set up role-plays. One involved members of the group playing the part of a parental figure, projecting their reactions and anxieties about the delinquent behaviour of a young member of their family and the impact of subsequent police involvement on the whole family. These sessions indicated an effective use of video techniques. Members of the group apparently enjoyed learning how to use a video camera. Their narrations in the role-plays seemed thoughtful and realistic. The staff made clear that the purpose of the role plays was to help those in the group appreciate that their offending not only affected their own lives, but also had an adverse impact on other members of their families.

These observations allow some more general comments to be made. First, it was clear that re-offending by members of the groups, and their subsequent remand in custody, posed great difficulties for the staff group. Specifically, the processes of group building and following an offending curriculum were considerably hampered. It is reasonable to assume that a pattern of re-offending by members of 'heavy end' groups was likely to continue. Staff indicated that young people referred to the Project were often already heavily involved in delinquency and, therefore, very unlikely immediately to relinquish offending.

A second general issue is at what stage young people fulfilling intermediate treatment and supervised activity requirements were, and/or ought to have been, taken back to court – on the grounds that they were unlikely to complete the terms of their order. It seems fair to argue that staff at the Speke Project were extremely reluctant to pursue breach proceedings. The 'heavy end' group staff believed that they could achieve better results ultimately by continuing to support and work with members of the group. It is also worth noting, though, that prior to the 1988 Criminal Justice Act there were no penalties available to the courts for breach of an intermediate treatment order, other than variation or discharge of the order. The 1988 Act, however, extended the sanctions available to the court to include a fine of up to £100 or an attendance centre order. New procedures following breach of a supervised activity order enable courts to pass any sentence, including a custodial sentence. At the end of the study, it remained to be seen what impact these new provisions would have on the use of breach proceedings by the Project.

The girls' group

Shirley   Shirley was 15. She had been in residential care, intermittently, since she was 11-years-old. Her mother's cohabitee was thought to be abusing Shirley. Her placement at the time of the study was in a home for teenage children in the city. Shirley was then in her final year at a Catholic comprehensive school. She attended school regularly and hoped to obtain some qualifications. She was referred to the Project by her social worker who hoped that the staff there might offer adult support and companionship to help Shirley through the crises of adolescence. Shirley was offered little supervision or stimulation at the children's home. Her social worker feared that Shirley's early experimentation with drugs might recommence if she did not have congenial interests and new friends to occupy her at least some evenings and weekends. Shirley was a faithful attender at the group meetings. At review meetings, her social worker and school year tutor both commented how much Shirley enjoyed, and benefited from, her membership of the girls' group. Staff at the Project felt rewarded by Shirley's enthusiasm.

Shirley, like Henry, is an invented character. Her experiences were, nonetheless, similar in many respects to those of some girls in the girls' group. The members of the girls' group, which ran from October 1987 to the end of May 1988, were in different legal and social situations from the members of the intermediate treatment group. Only one girl referred to the Project in the whole of the previous year had received a community-based sentence from the court. Generally, girls were referred to the Project by social workers for welfare reasons. As happens elsewhere, Project staff reported that local parents and other significant adults were relatively more concerned if girls, as compared with boys, stayed out late or did not attend school.

There were nine girls in the girls' group studied, mostly aged between 14 and 15 years. Five were experiencing very difficult personal circumstances. They were, at different stages of the group, living away from home in local authority care, about to enter care, or home on trial from a care placement. Social work agencies were heavily involved in their lives. For example, during the seven month life of the group, one of these girls lived in two foster placements, was made a ward of court, temporarily moved into the house of a relative and was finally placed in a children's home. The others led comparably unsettled lives. Staff at the Project could not alter the difficult circumstances of these young people's lives – what they could and did offer was steadfast, caring and affectionate support.

Two other girls in the group, whose names had recently been removed from the 'at risk' or child protection register, were referred to the group to receive a final stage of support as social work involvement with their respective families was ending. These two were both living at home. One was living in an apparently claustrophobic atmosphere as her mother was very reluctant to allow her to go out of the house for any social activities. These two had been referred to the group, therefore, almost as a social work finishing course! When she made the referrals, the social worker was closing the cases on the families but felt that joining the girls' group would help these two girls 'become their own people, [and especially for one of them] escape from Mum, acquire some social skills, mix with other young people'. The remaining two girls in the group were simply friends of other members and had been invited to make the process of joining a new group easier for the referred girls.

At the time of the fieldwork, there was a staff group of three for the group – two female project workers and the male project worker/ vehicle instructor. What the staff were trying to offer was a sympathetic forum for these girls, where sensitive and important issues could be discussed and where some group counselling and informal education could take place. The programme for the group included discussion sessions – for example, one evening the female police juvenile liaison officer talked to the group about issues of contraception, rape and sexism. Activity sessions, which the girls could select, were also offered – for example, the group went skating and dry slope skiing. In addition the girls participated in residential camps, one of which was an overnight camp sleeping under the stars.

During the life of the group, the five girls who were undergoing major upheavals in their lives took up an enormous amount of staff time and energy outside the group. These girls variously, absconded from care, changed care placements and experienced unsuccessful trial periods at home. The group offered a stable element in their lives to which they could return and where they would be accepted. Girls from this group who attended the nearby comprehensive school regularly dropped into the Project's coffee bar at lunch time. The impression gained by the researcher was that, for the girls whose lives were most disrupted, the group offered an important lifeline which they would be reluctant to leave. Indeed three of them, who were living close enough to do so, joined the successor group. As one commented:

'It's not like a palace nor nothing [but it] keeps you off the streets [and the groups should] go on for a full year...there is always someone to talk to if you have a problem...'

This girl had found support in the group and had also clearly enjoyed it. She felt that, whatever her problems, she was better off than some of the other girls in the group.

The group was apparently also important to a member who was living in more stable circumstances but who was lacking in social confidence. She remarked, enthusiastically:

'[The staff were] brilliant [and the group] helped me to mix with people. [I] was scared, helped a lot, [I wanted] to be equal with others not different, same as others.'

This girl who, because of her more stable home circumstances, perhaps had relied less on the group, also claimed to have found aspects of its organisation annoying. She enjoyed the group at the beginning but was occasionally bored as it wore on – she found too much time was sometimes spent discussing what to do the following week. She alleged that there was some pushing around or bullying in the group.

The work with the girls' group illustrates again the seemingly open-ended nature of much of the Project's work, and how staff seemed prepared to continue giving time and support to those who sought or needed it. The group scored a tangible success in persuading and supporting one shy member, whose circumstances did not warrant her being invited to another girls' group, to join the youth club at the Project.

The home on trial group

Bob   Bob was 13. His parents were divorced and he had moved home frequently. During the study he was living with his mother, who suffered periodic bouts of mental illness, and his siblings. His mother's boyfriend lived with the family intermittently. There had been recurring problems over Bob's schooling. Bob truanted persistently from his various, comprehensive schools but finally appeared to settle in a small, special school. He had spent a period in residential care when his mother was admitted to hospital. Before this, Bob was physically very neglected and was very withdrawn. He had no friends or outside interests and was left to look after himself. When his mother came home from hospital, Bob was also allowed home on trial. His social worker referred him to the Project to offer him some support until he was re-established at home. Bob came to the group fairly regularly and joined in all the activities. Home life was still somewhat bleak but Bob's physical appearance suggested he was better cared for. He opened up in the group and talked to the staff about his new-found interest in fishing. He joined the Project's fishing group run by one of the volunteers. The staff felt that Bob benefited from the continuing support and friendship of a group.

Bob is our last, hypothetical, but true-to-life, group member. The 'home on trial' group was run for a core group of ten, real life, youngsters – six boys and four girls. These were three groups of siblings and two other children, all of whom had been living away from home, though in one case for a very brief period. Two other children, one the sister of some of the children in the group, attended just a few sessions and another boy attended part of the group as a 'friend'. The group met between September 1987 and May 1988. The staff group up until Christmas consisted of a male project worker from the Project and a social worker from the district office; after Christmas, a female project worker replaced the social worker. A mature student on CQSW placement with the Education Welfare Service and a volunteer also helped with the group.

   The principal aim of the group was to provide support for young people who were re-establishing themselves at home after a period of separation in care. The age range of the group was quite wide – at the conclusion of the group the youngest member was 12-years-old and the oldest 15 years. The staff reported that this younger group had taken longer to settle than other groups at the Project. In the early stages there had been tantrums, arguments and incidents when brothers had bullied their step-sisters. The programme for the group was activity-oriented because the staff had found that the younger children quickly became bored and required much stimulation. The programme included:

- role plays;
- a local history session incorporating a visit to a churchyard;
- a stay in the country when the group walked down a mine and went on a night walk;
- visits to the ice rink;
- a group meal.

Project staff reported that, prior to being taken into care, an important cause for concern about these young people had been their non-attendance at school. But, as with the girls' group, the circumstances of individual children in the group varied enormously.

Some children in the group were perhaps the most deprived youngsters attending the Project. They were apparently physically and emotionally uncared for and suffered constant family upheavals – staff did not always know to which of several addresses they might be taking them 'home' at the end of a group session. The issue of whether these children should be returned to residential or foster care was being reviewed by social work staff during most of the study, but they were understandably reluctant to sanction re-admittance solely for absenteeism from school. The social workers' reasons for referring these children to the group had been, primarily, to obtain some adult interest and attention for them, which they lacked at home. The Project could provide this without the families being involved in another 'system'. The social workers felt that membership of the group had helped to maintain them in their homes. These youngsters all attended the group regularly and presumably, therefore, gained some enjoyment from it, but the researcher was unable to elicit much comment on this when she tried to talk to some of them. After the end of the series of group meetings, the family situations continued to be highly unstable and the Project maintained contact by inviting these particular youngsters to the summer camp run by the Project and involving them in a summer activities group.

Another boy who attended the group was re-admitted to care some months before the group ended. His membership of the group was interrupted when he spent time in the secure unit at an observation and assessment centre. By the end of the group meetings, he was in a placement at some distance from the Project.

For all the children, the group achieved its aim of offering some support over a difficult time in their lives. By the end of the group, at least half the members were more securely established at home.

Staff perspectives

The Speke Project's commitment to offering a community youth service in addition to a service to young offenders reflected, amongst other factors, the professional stance of the Project leader and his commitment to offering whatever help he could to young people living in a socially disadvantaged area. The Project leader described his and his staff's job as:

'...responding to need as they saw it...the balance is of giving a high priority to the group on IT orders whilst retaining energies and resources for kids (with other needs).'

The number of young people on orders referred to the Project by the courts varied over time but there was always capacity to undertake preventive work.

Because of the diversity of work at the Project, most staff undertook a mixture of delinquency-related and other work. It was evident, however, that staff perspectives, on the relative interest or importance of different elements of the Project's programme, varied. As noted already, the Project leader had general, community development objectives; the other staff evidently placed varying amounts of emphasis on juvenile justice work with the 'heavy end', care – or welfare – oriented work with girls or with other young people in difficulties, and the more general youth and community work.

Liaison with other agencies

Preceding sections have tried to indicate the range of groupwork at the Project. A common feature of 'treatment' groups run at the Project was a review process. Depending on the duration and nature of the group, up to three reviews of a young person's progress might take place, at the beginning, middle and end of a group. Review meetings were chaired by the Project leader, and the young person, their parent(s) and, when relevant, their area social worker, residential social worker and/or teacher were also invited to attend. The keyworker at the Project prepared a short report on the young people's involvement in the group, which always included some positive comments and recommendations for future action – whether or not the young person should be invited, or required, to join another group, for example. Reviews lasted half an hour and were intended to be informal in style. A short report on the proceedings was written by the keyworker.

The researcher observed reviews on several young people in each of the girls' and home on trial groups. She attended one 'heavy end' review – which the young person concerned did not attend. Some reviews were attended only by Project staff and other professionals, others were attended by the young person and/or a parent.

The Project staff laudably strove to prepare members of groups for these reviews to enable them to understand and participate in what was going on. The staff were aware that group members could be nervous and sometimes confused about what was being said or written about them, and about how this review procedure related to other reviews that might be taking place in their care or educational placements. Staff from other agencies were not always so sensitive and sometimes talked to each other, rather overlooking the young person present. The reactions of the young people to the reviews varied – for one girl, at a critical stage in her 'care career', the experience seemed nerve-wracking. But she, and others, though apprehensive at the outset, seemed boosted overall by the feedback and encouragement they received.

The juvenile justice system

A central issue in debates about juvenile justice is how to reduce the amount and degree of involvement which juveniles have with the formal processes of the juvenile justice system. Opportunities for diversion occur at different stages in a juvenile's delinquent career and can involve, variously, police, judicial and welfare agencies (Morris and Giller, 1987). A first objective, for some practitioners, is to divert juveniles from ever embarking on a delinquent career. Controversy as to the appropriateness of preventive intervention has already been discussed but it is an approach which has been endorsed by the Children Act 1989. For juveniles already engaged in delinquent activities, the second objective is to divert them from appearing in court. For juveniles who do appear in court, the third objective is to divert them from a custodial sentence.

The Speke Project was engaged in all three stages of the diversionary process. The youth club, activity groups and the Duke of Edinburgh award scheme could be defined as offering preventive programmes to young people living in the locality. The Project was certainly regarded as a preventive resource by local police representatives.

The main way that the Project was involved in diverting young people from the courts was via the Project's role in the juvenile liaison cautioning panel for the two social services districts in the south of the city. This panel was chaired by the Project leader, and meetings were initiated by the police juvenile liaison officer. They were attended also by probation, social services and education welfare staff. If they knew the young person already, these staff made a report to the meeting – if not, a member of the Project staff would visit the young person to assess whether community intervention, rather than a court hearing, seemed appropriate. In the 18-month period up to August 1988, the panel considered 19 referrals, all boys, for relatively minor offences. Agreement was reached to caution all the youngsters referred, the majority with some kind of condition attached. The Project leader was confident that none of those cautioned had re-offended during the 18-month period.

The Project leader noted that the number of referrals to the panel was rather lower than anticipated. It was suggested to the researcher, by some observers, that this was because the panel was only consulted if the police felt that the caution should be conditional or that there were welfare concerns. Certainly, when the panel agreed on a caution it was often the case that a condition was attached. The reason given by the Project leader was:

'Generally a common sense condition will be added to the recommendation of a caution, in view of the fact that all those referred will have had an official or unofficial (if under 10 years old) caution previously.'

During the research, conflicting views were expressed about the way the panel ought to operate. Some favoured the status quo. Others, arguing from a justice perspective, suggested that welfare criteria should not be a deciding factor (assuming that they were) as to whether or not a case was referred to the cautioning panel.

Furthermore, the view was expressed that as many *unconditional* cautions, or no further action decisions, should be made by the panel as possible. It was feared that young people receiving conditional cautions were, in effect, being drawn further than was warranted into the criminal justice system.

Concerning the third of the three possible diversionary stages, the Project acted in several ways to ensure that young people already in the court process were diverted from custody. The bail support scheme, to enable youngsters who might otherwise be remanded in custody to remain in the community, and the supervised activity order and intermediate treatment programmes have been discussed already. Another strand in the strategy for diverting young people from custodial care was the panel system operated by the social work districts in collaboration with the Project.

The social services panels, to which the Project sent representatives, were chaired and attended by district social workers. The aim of the panels was to act as a gatekeeping device – to ensure that strict and consistent criteria were applied in making recommendations about sentencing, such that non-custodial options were available to as many young people as possible. Thus, the tasks of the panels were to monitor the information included in social enquiry reports and the recommendations made to the courts. An example raised a number of times during the research was that reference to a young person's voluntary attendance at the intermediate treatment Project was omitted, if magistrates were likely to regard such involvement as suggesting that the community-based sentencing option had already failed – such a suggestion might encourage them to award a higher tariff sentence.

Incidentally, the panel meetings had the broader role of offering the Project and social services district staff a forum for the exchange of information and debate about issues of shared concern in juvenile justice. Further opportunity for such broader discussions occurred at fortnightly meetings, held at the Project, which were chaired and attended by Project staff and which members from both social services district panels attended.

In addition to their input to social enquiry reports via the panel system, Project staff also prepared their own reports for the court, outlining their recommendations for disposal based on assessment work they had undertaken with young people at the Project. Project staff often accompanied youngsters to court and spoke on their behalf, a time-consuming commitment. We know that it is in young people's best interests to remain out of custody. The Project staff made determined efforts to achieve this objective.

Care-related work and collaborative working

Decisions about what groups to run in addition to the 'heavy end' group were made by Project staff, following discussion about perceived needs with colleagues in the social services districts and the education welfare service. One forum for such discussion was the annual review meeting, attended by representatives from these agencies. For example, at the review meeting held during the study, education welfare staff identified a number of children posing school attendance problems, and the possibility of the EWOs running a group for some of these children with back-up from Project staff was mooted. Decisions about new groups were also based on the experience of running existing groups. Thus, staff felt that several of the girls' group would benefit from continued membership of such a group. Once a decision to run a group had been made, Project staff set out their objectives and sought specific referrals from the relevant agencies.

The young people in the 'voluntary treatment' groups were, then, generally known to other welfare agencies and, as noted in the descriptions of the groups, some were living in residential institutions – a children's home or an observation and assessment centre. Project staff liaised with the staff at these establishments to enable these young people to participate in the programmes at the Project.

Youngsters living in residential institutions obviously have to abide by their rules. During the study, this seemed to pose no problem for youngsters attending the Project from children's homes or the education department's residential schools in the city. However, difficulty did arise over the rule enforced by the girls' Observation and Assessment centre – if youngsters absconded, they were not allowed to attend outside activities for seven days after their return. Staff mediated with this centre on behalf of a member of the girl's group, who absconded on a number of occasions, and whom the Observation and Assessment centre staff were reluctant to send to the Speke Project before the end of the prescribed seven days. The Observation and Assessment centre staff argued that the intermediate treatment Project was offering an inducement which other young people in their care did not receive and that it was not appropriate to bend the rules for this purpose. The Project staff's plausible response was that they were offering a treatment programme, not a positive reinforcement for running away, and that the programme could not be run effectively if girls were not allowed to attend. In this particular instance, the girl was allowed to attend the group. Furthermore, staff at the intermediate treatment Project continued to press for a change of policy on the issue and some measures were taken by social services management to remedy such difficulties. This example indicates again the strength of commitment of the girls' group staff to the young people with whom they worked and their belief in the treatment programmes they had developed.

Perspectives of other agencies

It was evident that outside agencies varied in their assessments of the work and achievements of the Speke Project. During the study, the researcher interviewed 14 representatives from agencies who collaborated with the Project or who worked, in other spheres, with some of the same youngsters. Seven of those interviewed worked in the two social work districts in the south of the city.

Those talked to clearly had 'lots of praise' for, and 'honoured the work done' by, the Project – 'it's a brilliant resource', said one. Many comments were made on how staff at the Project persevered with difficult adolescents in the 'heavy end' groups and apparently 'remained buoyant' – 'they seemed to bounce back despite repeatedly [being] faced with re-offending'. The motor project was seen to offer an imaginative and constructive response to vehicle crime.

There were, however, some issues on which the opinions of these representatives diverged. These were:

- the range of work it was thought appropriate for the Project to undertake;
- aspects of the manner in which work was undertaken;
- the location and use of the building. Each of these important areas will now be discussed in turn.

What exactly should the Project be doing?

The Project's work divided broadly into:

- work undertaken with young offenders;

- work undertaken in treatment groups with other disadvantaged youngsters;
- broader youth work through the youth club, activity groups and Duke of Edinburgh scheme;
- some community development work via, for example, the use of local volunteers, the monthly lunch club for professionals working in the locality and the support offered for local initiatives, like the victims' support scheme.

According to their own professional work and interests, the representatives from other agencies who were interviewed were familiar with one or more of these areas of work.

Mixed views were expressed about the wide range of work undertaken by the Project, about how the different areas of work were managed and inter-related, and about how the breadth of work was viewed by other significant bodies. Responses graduated, fairly evenly, from unconditional approval that the Project accepted a wide range of referrals, involved local volunteers and offered a variety of opportunities for local youth 'in a fairly run down area' to a slightly more reluctant and conditional acceptance of the Project's broad-based approach.

Conditional approval rested, for example, on ensuring:

- that work with the 'heavy end' was not adversely affected by this broad range of activities;
- that the Project made clear its objectives in its work with each 'client' group;
- that, where relevant, the referring agency and the Project shared common objectives.

The need for work with the 'heavy end' to be distinguished from work with other groups was also stressed – for two reasons. Some respondents thought that the Project was synonymous in the eyes of the local community with 'bad lads', and there was a danger that other young people attending the Project could be similarly tarnished – with potentially damaging consequences – if the different strands of work and different target groups, were not clearly delineated. Incidentally, this was the reverse side of the concern expressed by the Project leader that the 'heavy end' group members would be 'labelled' as delinquent in the eyes of the community if the Project did not include broader youth activities.

The second reason for distinguishing between the different groups being run was that magistrates might draw the conclusion that intermediate treatment had been tried, and failed, with young people who had attended the Project but had not been in a 'heavy end' group. Alternatively, magistrates might seek to formalise what they regarded as existing involvement, by making intermediate treatment or supervised activity order requirements – even if these were not appropriate disposals. As has already been noted, these concerns were shared by the Project staff, who often avoided references in court reports to a young person's previous involvement in Project activities.

Some additional reservations about the broad range of work at the Project were based on (sometimes inaccurate) comparisons with the more narrow focus of work at other intermediate treatment Projects in the city. Implied criticism of the Project on this count, however, was balanced by acknowledgement that, whether or not the work was strictly the province of an intermediate treatment project, the work with girls (and other youngsters) to avoid, ameliorate or bring to an end a residential care placement, was laudable. Further, it could be seen to fall within the authority's guidelines for additional areas of work that intermediate treatment centres in the city might undertake at their discretion, when faced with a demonstrable need and sufficient spare resources to meet that need.

Service delivery

Attention here has focused mainly on the way that treatment groups were managed. Outside agencies had very different levels of knowledge about what was offered to young people who attended groups and some took for granted satisfactory levels of service delivery. Those with more detailed knowledge of work in the Project also expressed their trust in the abilities of the staff group – though some distinctions were made between the experience of different staff. In particular, the relative efficiency of different staff was commented upon as regards:

- setting, communicating and adhering to group objectives;
- maintaining control;
- ensuring that there was adequate debriefing after each session and at the end of the life of each group, involving all staff members in discussion on the strengths and weaknesses of the group.

There was, nonetheless, virtually unanimous sympathy and admiration declared for the way that staff persevered with difficult and unreliable youths, supported them in court, and persisted in negotiating with the 'heavy end' to establish some kind of working relationship. 'Negotiated everything is about right these days', commented one observer. Yet there were some doubts also as to whether sufficient control and discipline were always maintained, and occasional examples were given of instances when those interviewed felt that Project staff had not been able to exert control over a group, with consequent damage to premises. Several queried whether staff persevered too long with youngsters who were thought (by some) to deserve custodial sentences.

A suitable site?

Many comments were passed on the fortification of the building. Where opinion differed was on whether one building could serve all the purposes it was intended to meet. To return to the issues of contamination and labelling already discussed, one suggestion made was that the youth and community activities should take place in a separate building from the treatment groups. Others discounted notions of contamination, on the grounds that the youngsters lived in the same locality and attended the same schools.

Secondly, it was queried whether the location of the Project in the centre of Speke estate was compatible with offering a service to nearly the whole of the south of the city. To reach the Project from some parts of the catchment area, youngsters had to catch two buses and Project staff often undertook the time-consuming task of ferrying youngsters to and from the Project. Such transport arrangements were additional to those which had to be made for young people living in the Observation and Assessment centres in the north of the city. It was suggested that Project staff were unlikely to acquire the same knowledge about local circumstances and families in the more distant parts of the catchment area, that they had absorbed about the district in which the Project was situated.

Conclusion

This chapter offers a descriptive account of work at the Speke Project during the time of the research study. As with the two projects whose work has already been described, the impact of the Speke Project has been explored in discussions with staff at the Project, the staff of other key agencies and, to a degree, with young people at the Project.

The Speke Project provided the broadest range of service provision of the three projects, encompassing juvenile justice work, treatment groups with girls and other groups of young people with specifically defined problems, as well as youth and community work.

The breadth of work undertaken at the Project was the source of a division of views amongst key observers. On the one hand were those who believed that the service offered by an intermediate treatment centre should, above all, concentrate on work with convicted offenders. Yet, in practice, proponents of this view also welcomed the services and resources offered to girls, and to other youngsters at risk of care, because such resources would likely otherwise not have been available to these groups. What they expressed reservations about was the appropriateness of all these services being offered under one roof. Others believed that an intermediate treatment centre can legitimately offer a broad range of services, including preventive and youth and community services, in an area where other community facilities were limited and where many, very 'hard-pressed' families lived.

During the study Project staff experienced some difficulty in obtaining the cooperation of members of the 'heavy-end' group. This has to be set in the context of the considerable self-discipline required, over a reasonably long period, to fulfil the requirements of a community-based sentence.

What was evident was the admiration expressed by a number of interested parties, for the commitment of staff to persevere with young people. Well aware of the disadvantages and deprivations experienced by many of their customers, the staff displayed consistent sympathy and understanding.

8. Matching models with practice in intermediate treatment

The principal concern in this chapter is to contrast the models and approaches portrayed in earlier chapters with the work of the three case study centres. Two of the models discussed – those of welfare and justice – have shaped much of the debate about young people in trouble in recent years. Two other perspectives, which focus on more specific issues – the developmental and corporatist approaches – were also described. It is suggested here that the four models and approaches in combination provide a framework for classifying and understanding the case study centres. The combined classification may have a broader application inasmuch as it includes developments in intermediate treatment which took place in the 1980s.

A combination of models

Models are simplified descriptions of reality. By illustrating key relationships, they help us to make sense of the world and, also, to make predictions, – to ask questions about why things are as they are, and how they might change. An everyday example is the use ramblers make of scale 'models' of the countryside, more usually called ordinance survey maps, to plan their walks. As changes occur – a farmer bars access across a field, a new housing development is built – the maps become less accurate and less useful. The publication of new editions, incorporating such changes, restores the value of the maps.

The models and approaches discussed in this chapter highlight important features of policy and practice in intermediate treatment. Their value in this study is in helping to pinpoint prominent aspects of the work of the case-study projects for the purposes of comparison and evaluation. Conversely, the case studies also serve to test the validity of the models and approaches and, in a modest way, can be used to modify them.

Table 8.1 summarises which models and approaches were evident in the work of the North City, Boughton Hall and Speke centres. The classifications are based on the descriptions which the project workers themselves have offered of their work and on the researcher's observations, as presented in Chapters 5, 6 and 7. The table suggests that none of the projects could be adequately described by a single model or approach. Each centre was, nevertheless, distinctive – each, it is argued, is best described by a different combination of these models and approaches.

Table 8.1 Models describing the work of the three case study centres

	North City	Boughton Hall	Speke
Welfare	No	Yes	Yes
Justice	Yes	Yes	Yes
Developmental	No	Yes	Yes
Corporatist	Yes	No	Yes

A sample of three centres cannot, of course, provide a firm basis for developing more complex models. Nonetheless, the findings of this research study certainly indicate some characteristics of current practice in intermediate treatment which future models of practice are likely to have to accommodate.

In summary, it is argued that all three, case-study centres displayed characteristics of the 'justice' model. Different 'pairs' of projects are judged, additionally, to have adopted the other approaches – Boughton Hall and Speke the 'welfare' and 'developmental' approaches, and North City and Speke a 'corporatist' approach. It is worth explaining and justifying these classifications in a little more detail, with reference to the objectives and work of the projects.

The first model in Table 8.1, that of 'welfare', regards delinquent and troubled adolescents as the products of deprived environments. This model was not observed to influence significantly the work undertaken with young offenders at any of the centres. Where the 'welfare' approach was evident was in the alternative-to-care work undertaken at Speke and Boughton Hall, where laudable attempts were made to combat the impact of socially and economically disadvantaged environments on the lives of young people.

Secondly, the justice model; this approach, it will be recalled, defines criminal acts in terms of opportunity and rational choice. Offenders should be held accountable for their actions. However, their punishment should not be disproportionate to the crime, nor based on judgements about the home circumstances and/or welfare of the young person. During the research, staff at all three centres broadly accepted this definition of their work with young offenders. In particular, staff were generally anxious to avoid unnecessary, and potentially damaging, interventions in the lives of young people following offending.

Of the three centres, North City was most consistent in its practice in this matter. The project dealt only with known offenders and the project leader and her staff were in agreement over approved methods of work. At Boughton Hall and Speke, the customer population included significant numbers of young people with no convictions. The justice orientation of these centres was, therefore, somewhat diluted.

Two examples indicate how the 'justice' approach could be blunted. During the research study, Boughton Hall staff occasionally offered in court to undertake additional work with young people appearing before the bench, to supplement a low-tariff sentence. Such discretionary intervention by intermediate treatment workers could be interpreted as infringing the principles of a strict justice approach. Furthermore, one criticism made of the work of the Speke cautioning panel, chaired by the project leader, was that it too readily recommended conditional cautions, when a higher proportion of 'no further action' or 'straight' cautions would have been outcomes more in accordance with a 'justice' approach (see Blagg, 1985).

The ideas embodied in the third, 'developmental', approach informed programmes of work at Boughton Hall and Speke. Staff at these centres, assuming that the vast majority of young people would grow out of their offending and other problems, placed a high priority on upholding and strengthening the links between young people and their communities. Young people would thus be helped to avoid damaging their future education and employment chances as well as their emotional welfare.

At Boughton Hall the lessons of the developmental approach were contained in the Project leader's early appraisal paper. This discussed how the weakening of social bonds contributed to delinquency and advocated the practice of fostering the links which young people had with their communities. Problems typically experienced by young people were at school and/or on entering the labour market. The Project leader's objectives were to offer support during transitional periods while young people overcame their problems, and to forge links with agencies, especially schools, to offer whatever support was feasible to sustain a young person in the community. One of the objectives of the Speke project was to help anyone referred who 'was experiencing difficulties with life and the problems of adolescence'. In practice, this frequently meant long-term involvement with young people. The Speke staff, like those at Boughton Hall, collaborated with schools and other agencies to offer additional support to young people at some risk of entering the care of the local authority. Thus, during the field work, project staff were working with education social work staff to set up a group for young people who were absenting themselves from school.

An important focus of the last approach, 'corporatism', is the trend towards administrative, rather than judicial, decision-making for dealing with young offenders. In two of the case study projects, 'administrative' decisions were taken as described by the corporatist model. Thus, in the two Liverpool projects, representatives of different professional groups met at cautioning and juvenile panels to reach a consensus as to what response should be made to young people's offending.

The North City and Speke cautioning panel meetings, attended by project staff, district social workers, education and police personnel, met to consider particular cases and to assess whether these young people should be recommended for a conditional caution. Decisions were reached on the basis of information already known, or specially obtained, by different panel members. For example, social workers might contribute information about families known to them which was recorded on their departmental files. Young people did not attend the meetings but learnt the outcome of the cautioning panel when, for example, they were subsequently required to attend the intermediate treatment centre after a caution had been administered. The, wholly worthwhile, objective of the panel discussions was to slow young people's progress through the tariff of penalties. The point at issue here is that the procedures used illustrate the development of administrative decision-making with regard to young offenders.

Another example of administrative decision-making was at the juvenile panels for reviewing social enquiry report recommendations. Such panels were attended by the staff of the two Liverpool projects and by relevant social services district staff. Again, young people and/or their families did not attend these meetings but the decisions reached were discussed with them. The panels can be regarded as decision-making forums since it is known that social enquiry report recommendations significantly influence court sentencing (Stafford and Hill, 1987), although not always for the reasons the report writer intended. (Parker, Sumner and Jarvis, 1989)

The four main models were, then, readily identifiable in the work of the centres. The approach described in Chapter 4 as a variant of the 'welfare' model, that of 'treatment', has not been identified separately here. This approach assumes that offending, and other 'disturbed' behaviour, is caused by underlying psychological problems. The problems of some individuals were described to the researcher as possibly rooted in personality disorders and there were occasional discussions, at Speke in particular, as to whether individual young people would benefit from the proffered help of a psychologist. In practice, however, the work observed with these young people was, as with others, largely focused on helping them to cope with the legal, economic and social realities of their lives.

It is worth acknowledging that there is, to some degree, an arbitrary element in classifying the case study projects. The complex patterns of their work cannot be portrayed fully by the typology. For example, as we have seen, the Boughton Hall project has not been classified as 'corporatist'. This is mainly because there were no juvenile or cautioning panels operating in Chester. Discussions did, however, take place between project staff, social workers and the police as to how individual young people should be dealt with. The view taken here is that informal collaboration of this kind should not be described as 'corporatism'. To take a second example, the North City project has been excluded from the 'developmental' category. This classification reflects the project's specific focus on the juvenile justice system. This is not to deny, however, the project staff's commitment to maintaining young offenders in their communities, and their belief that most of these young people will 'grow out' of offending.

What is evident is that the theoretical and practice models underpinning work in the three centres were complex. This finding accords with the account of developments in intermediate treatment offered in Chapter 4. It certainly confirms that it is simplistic to assume that the much-rehearsed justice/welfare debate adequately summarises all controversy in intermediate treatment. Yet, the four models identified as particularly influencing the work of the case-study centres do, **in combination**, provide a framework for beginning to understand the particular orientation of each centre and for comparing and contrasting the three centres.

Other influential variables

Clearly, though, the four models identified as influencing the work of these centres cannot account for all aspects of the projects' organisation. In considering the development of the case-study centres it is useful to consider other, influential factors such as:

- the early history of intermediate treatment;
- relevant government legislation;
- initiatives and trends in community care.

It can be seen that the Speke centre's 'preventive' programmes echo early concerns in intermediate treatment. A government circular in 1977 stated:

'The expression "intermediate treatment" can be used...to describe arrangements for helping children and young people in trouble or at risk, or thought to be at risk of getting into trouble. The concern is to help those concerned to overcome their difficulties and fulfil their potential.' (DHSS, 1977, Intermediate Treatment Circular, 27 January)

The North City project wasthe product of the 1982 Criminal Justice Act and the subsequent DHSS LAC(83) initiative. Boughton Hall's premises became available as the trend away from residential care, and towards care in the community, led to the closure of a former children's home.

Another influential element has been Barnardo's management philosophy. This has enabled the three centres to develop in different ways, in response to perceived local needs. Thus the line manager in Barnardo's responsible for the three study projects has explained that the baseline for all the charity's work is its childcare aim

'To provide and develop, in consultation with statutory and other agencies, and in partnership with parents, selected services for children and young people in need and their families on a regional basis. These services, by their nature and by evaluation of their effectiveness, should endeavour to extend knowledge and practice.'

Within the parameters of this aim, Barnardo's seeks to cooperate with local authorities and other agencies to develop appropriate child care provision. In establishing the three intermediate treatment centres included in this study, the charity negotiated with the two local authorities concerned to achieve mutually-agreed management objectives. This is not, of course, the whole story. Local authority objectives change and projects develop particular areas of expertise. Barnardo's management, therefore, keeps its projects under review – attempting to ensure that their objectives and those of the local authority remain in accord. The research project reported here has been one element in this process.

Conclusion

This chapter has drawn on the models of intermediate treatment practice elaborated in earlier chapters in order to analyse in greater detail, and highlight the distinctive approaches of, the three study centres. It has been argued that combinations of the original models and approaches are required to describe current practice in the three centres accurately. Furthermore, the combined classification may help provide a better understanding of developments generally in the field of intermediate treatment.

Finally, Chapter 9 will draw together the main conclusions of the whole research programme and suggest some ways these might inform debate about future directions in juvenile justice.

9. Conclusions

Barnardo's principal aims in commissioning the programme of research on intermediate treatment reported in this book were that the results would contribute to the development of policy and practice, and would help Barnardo's evaluate its own role, as a voluntary organisation providing intermediate treatment services.

The first task in this concluding chapter is to consider how the evidence from the three case studies can contribute to key questions and debates in intermediate treatment. The second focus in the chapter is how Barnardo's role in providing intermediate treatment services is perceived by some of the staff from other agencies with which Barnardo's project staff collaborates. Thirdly, and finally, the chapter discusses the use Barnardo's North-West Division has made of the research results in negotiations with local authorities about the future development of the case study projects.

A return to the key debates

Two fundamental questions about intermediate treatment were posed in Chapter 1 – why is there such a range of practice activity, and what are the goals which practitioners hope to achieve? It has been suggested that answers are rooted in the historical and legislative contexts of intermediate treatment. As we saw in Chapter 2, these set two somewhat different goals for intermediate treatment:

- to promote the well-being of young people with problems, in other words, a welfare-oriented function;
- to offer a service to the juvenile courts by organising community-based sentencing options.

The models of policy and practice which have developed in response to these original tasks were outlined in Chapter 4. The descriptions of the models and approaches in that chapter ended with some questions about each and these, taken collectively, summarise some of the main debates surrounding intermediate treatment. The contribution which the evidence of the case studies can make to these debates will be considered now.

A commitment to welfare

Two of the three case study projects, Boughton Hall and Speke, offered alternative-to-care programmes based on the principles of the 'welfare' model. What value did project staff and young people place upon these programmes? Was there any evidence of 'net widening', in which it could it be judged that the work of the projects was, in any way, infringing the civil liberties of young people? How did the staff of other key agencies view these programmes?

The practitioner standpoint The premise of the 'welfare' approach, in essence, is that young people's problems are largely attributable to their disadvantaged environment. The practice task is to improve the environment or circumstances of those affected.

At all the case study projects, the first priority was work with young offenders and this was conducted according to 'justice' principles – that is that the punishment should be proportionate to the offence. Practitioners at Boughton Hall and Speke were, therefore, familiar with the 'justice-welfare' debate and the criticisms levelled at the 'welfare' approach. Indeed, a minority of staff at these two projects expressed reservations about the broad-based nature of their projects' programmes. Motivation for the 'welfare' approach was, however, supplied by commitment to alleviating the effects of severe poverty and disadvantage which, certainly in Speke, were experienced by many young people. More pragmatically, the project leaders argued that there was insufficient juvenile justice work to justify the staffing and resources currently obtaining.

The 'welfare' approach was put into practice in the care-related programmes. The projects sought referrals to these programmes from social workers. At Speke details of a planned group, such as a girls' group, were circulated to the social services district staff. The criteria for membership of groups would be stated, though sometimes these were relaxed to include some friends of those referred.

Staff running care-related groups at Speke during the study affirmed that, in their view, the groups offered a worthwhile service to young people, almost all of whom had suffered serious upheavals in their lives.

At Boughton Hall, the content and duration of the more intensive, care-related work was negotiated with the social worker and young person at the time of referral. The main criterion for a referral was that the social worker judged there to be a significant risk of the young person entering the care of the local authority. The role of the Boughton Hall staff was to help to reduce that risk and avert entry into care. It was recognised by project staff that social workers varied in their judgements as to whether – and when – to make a referral. For this reason the project leader was beginning to develop more specific referral criteria.

Project staff had a genuine commitment to meeting welfare needs. They seemed confident that they were helping to fill a gap in provision for young people. There was, though, agreement amongst the staff that the grounds for referral, and the goals of the intervention, had not always been specified clearly enough.

Young people's perspectives The conclusions here have to be interpreted in the knowledge that:

- not all the young people asked were prepared to talk to the researcher;
- those who did talk were not always very forthcoming;
- their comments were certainly not framed in terms of the 'justice/ welfare' debate;
- it is not known how they moderated their views in efforts to please the researcher.

Their expressed views could, though, be considered alongside their attendance and demeanour at the projects – always remembering that these were known to be affected by, for example, serious disruptions in their personal lives.

These limitations accepted, there were clear examples of young people welcoming and deriving benefit from care-related programmes. Perhaps the best illustration coming from the case studies is the lifeline the Speke girls' group offered to many of its members. A number of young people at Boughton Hall, experiencing problems at home, school or work, also welcomed and relied quite significantly upon the support that was offered.

'Net-widening' Critics of the 'welfare' approach have argued that young people participating in 'preventive' intermediate treatment, if subsequently convicted of offending, risk receiving more severe sentences from the courts than their offences would warrant. An implication of the argument is that young people who have already come to official notice are more likely to be convicted than those who have not.

The project leaders at both Speke and Boughton Hall argued that they had no experience of attendance at their projects inadvertently leading to offending. They refuted the possibility of 'contamination', as a result of non-offenders mixing with known offenders at the centres, on the grounds that many of the young people met elsewhere – at school or in their neighbourhoods. This assurance did not convince all those who made referrals. Some social workers expressed their reluctance to make referrals to the care-related programmes because of the presence of known offenders at the projects. There was a fear of placing young people with problems at yet a further disadvantage. It was thought that in the community, if not in the courts, their association with a centre for offenders would lead to their reputations being tarnished.

No direct evidence was found during the study of courts passing more severe sentences simply because young people had had a prior association with one of the projects. Project staff, however, acted to reduce this likelihood by giving serious consideration as to whether mention would be made of care-related work in any court report. Outside the court process, the comments of school staff did suggest that acceptance onto a project programme was taken as final proof that a young person was indeed exhibiting severe behavioural problems and would be likely to continue to cause difficulties in school.

Civil liberties A further criticism directed at welfare-oriented programmes is that open-ended intervention may infringe a young person's civil liberties. This was not observed to apply in the case studies. Young people's involvement in the main programmes was normally planned beforehand, and reviewed regularly – with the cooperation of the young person, a parent or other adult carer and representatives of the referring agencies. There was one example in the study of a project programme being extended beyond its original life on a somewhat *ad hoc* basis and social services district staff were disparaging about the organisation of this particular programme. However, they did not link this lack of forward planning, and nor would the researcher, with any loss of young people's civil rights in this instance.

The researcher encountered no truly reluctant participants on the welfare-based programmes. She did meet several young people at Speke and Boughton Hall who tried to elicit her help in increasing their opportunities to attend the projects!

The referring agencies Field social workers and their managers who were committed to a 'welfare' approach welcomed the resources and expertise these projects could offer to young people in difficulties. Some, though, acknowledged that the relatively broad criteria for entry to some care-related programmes were contrary to current practice emphasis on focused intervention.

Social workers who advocated a 'justice' model naturally expressed some reservations about the broad-based approach adopted at Boughton Hall and Speke. Yet even they praised some of the care-related work, particularly that undertaken with girls. Their provisos were that such work should have clearly stated goals and well-structured plans for achieving them.

School staff, education's social work staff and police representatives judged the projects in the light of their own agency objectives. Thus school staff appraisals of the projects' work were linked with the subsequent attendance and behaviour of pupils in school. Overall, school staff had a high esteem for the work of the projects but their judgements about what had, or could be, achieved with individual pupils were not always optimistic.

The police welcomed the preventive work of the centres, with which they were often closely associated, and which accorded in their estimation with their efforts in crime prevention.

Conclusion What main conclusions may be drawn, then, about the 'welfare' approach as implemented at two of the case study projects? Such programmes, it seems, can offer help and support to some young people who would not otherwise receive help. The programmes generally agreed to be of most value are those with a defined target group, clearly stated objectives and a structured programme geared to the experiences of the recipients. Measures should be taken to ensure that participation in such programmes is not allowed to influence how any subsequent offending is dealt with. Although not unanimously endorsed, there was very strong support for preventive and care-related programmes being organised quite separately from programmes for known offenders.

Managing justice

All three case study projects incorporated 'justice' principles into their work with young offenders. These principles define offending as freely-chosen but stipulate that punishment should not be disproportionate to the offence. It should be taken into account that much juvenile offending is comparatively petty, that most young people 'grow out' of offending and that the experience of custody can be highly damaging. Young people, on the whole, fare best when allowed to remain in their communities.

The questions considered here are about the organisation, targeting and outcomes of programmes devised in accordance with 'justice' principles. Also discussed are the effects of monitoring and intervening in the juvenile justice system.

The lessons of the case studies are necessarily limited but can, nevertheless, contribute to the wider debate. It is possible to compare the work of North City, funded initially with LAC(83) funding and dealing *solely* with known offenders, with the work of the two projects which ran programmes for young offenders alongside those for young people with no known involvement in offending.

Careful targeting The evidence of the case studies suggested that at North City the programmes were more tightly managed and targeted than at the other projects. Some examples can be given to support this assertion.

North City's practice of organising programmes for individuals rather than groups enabled the project to insist that young people started to fulfil the requirements of their sentences the very day that these were passed by the courts. This immediate start was not always enforced during the study at the other projects. Delays could, and did, occur between the time the courts passed sentence and the time young people started to complete the terms of their orders.

At North City, only those complying with the terms of an intermediate treatment or supervised activity requirement had to undertake the 'offending curriculum' exercises. Others – for example young people awaiting a court hearing – were not expected to do so, though some chose to take part. At the other projects, the exact status of known offenders and, consequently, their legal obligations were not always as clearly defined. As we saw, not all the young people in Speke's 'heavy-end' group were fulfilling a court order. Yet all were, effectively, bound by the same group procedures – though not, of course, subject to the same legal sanctions for non-compliance. At Boughton Hall, as some young people came near to completing their court orders, staff explained to the researcher that these young men would be encouraged to join a further programme, a 'leaving-care' group. This additional programme was highly relevant to them. The suggestion was described to the researcher, however, in a way that left unresolved whether the young men concerned would appreciate that their further participation in project programmes would be wholly voluntary.

A final issue concerning face-to-face work with young people deserves consideration. Proponents of the 'justice' approach have censured unnecessary and intrusive interventions solely on welfare grounds. They do not, though, imply that a young person's problems should be ignored. Although welfare problems were never the primary reason for intervention at North City, they were always taken seriously by the staff. During the study, guidance was offered to young people on health, employment and social security issues. This was also the case at the other two projects. Providing caring, patient help was a feature of work at all three centres.

Gate-keeping Management of the juvenile justice system paralleled the work undertaken directly with young people. At North City, where project staff were largely responsible for the city's statistical monitoring system, this area of work was assigned high priority and seemed to yield results. The highest rate of intermediate treatment requirements in Liverpool was recorded in 1988 for young people from the district served by the project – and in 1989, there was a remarkable nil custody rate in this district.

Efforts to intervene in the juvenile justice system cannot be undertaken by a project working in isolation. The North City Project's work was fully supported and assisted by the policies of the local social services district manager. The other two projects were also active, in different ways, in managing the juvenile justice system. The Speke staff played an active role in the local juvenile and cautioning panels; while Boughton Hall's project leader helped produce the monitoring statistics for Chester City. These efforts were less comprehensive than at North City and, certainly as far as Boughton Hall was concerned, had in the past received less back-up from the local social services management. As recorded in Chapter 6, before the recent district reorganisation, Chester Social Services District management had favoured a 'welfare' approach. There are, then, some difficulties in comparing the effectiveness of the efforts of the three projects. For example, despite the absence of a cautioning panel, Chester District had the highest cautioning rate in the county. It does seem clear, nevertheless, that the consistent system management activities at North City had a distinct impact on sentencing outcomes.

Conclusion In conclusion, at all three projects staff advocated the 'justice' model as appropriate in dealing with young offenders. The approach was implemented more rigorously, however, at North City where both project staff and local social services management were wholeheartedly committed to the approach. In other words, the case studies give some reason to believe that at centres which work exclusively with known offenders, and where the district management is supportive, there will be a sharper focus on, more punctilious management of, and better results in the juvenile justice work.

Developmental strategies

A central plank of the 'developmental' approach is that most young people grow out of offending and other behavioural difficulties. This is stressed equally by upholders of the 'justice' model. The practice implications of each model, however, differ. The key issue in implementing the 'developmental' approach is how to strengthen the work of the institutions in our society which are normally responsible for young people – these include families, schools, and residents of local communities.

The questions raised earlier about this approach were:

• how had it influenced practice at the projects;
• what were the goals of relevant programmes and which young people were included in them;
• how successful were the projects in sustaining young people in their communities;

- was the intervention proportional to the scale of difficulties young people were experiencing?

Some of these questions resemble those asked about the welfare model. This is because the 'developmental' approach is also open to the charge that it may lead to unnecessary social control being exerted over the lives of young people.

Various strategies consistent with the 'developmental' approach were implemented at Boughton Hall and Speke during the research study. These were applied primarily in programmes for those with behavioural problems. Thus at Boughton Hall programmes were run for school refusers and the Project maintained links with local secondary schools, Education's social work service and local employers. Youth club and other activity group provision was offered to young people on the fringes of care or of offending and local volunteers were involved in running such activities.

The ethos of the 'developmental' approach was most elaborately expressed in the Boughton Hall project leader's appraisal paper, which referred to the vulnerability of adolescents experiencing difficulties at school and on entering the job market, and which discussed methods for strengthening young people's links with the wider community and for developing their sense of social responsibility. The appraisal paper was written to discuss the project's approach for dealing with known offenders. During the study, however, at Boughton Hall and Speke, developmental methods were most frequently adopted with those on care-related programmes.

The experience of the case studies suggested that the work undertaken by project staff supporting young people in their communities was valued by many of the young people. The projects were not always successful in maintaining young people in their own homes. The staff did, though, sustain their contact with, and support of, those who were taken into the care of the local authority. Staff also helped young people resume their lives in the community when they left care. No evidence was apparent during the studies to suggest that intervention was prolonged beyond the wishes of either the young person or his or her family. To illustrate this, when one family informed project staff that their problems with their son were largely resolved, the family, project and school staff agreed that the young man should cease to attend the project.

The indications of the case studies allayed some of the doubts expressed in the review of this approach in Chapter 4. The project interventions were reviewed regularly and revised agreements formulated, as appropriate, with the families and agencies concerned. Such arrangements are clearly essential if the interests of the young people concerned are to be safeguarded.

Corporate decisions

The last perspective, 'corporatism', does not proffer an explanation of adolescent problems, nor prescribe policy and practice solutions. It focuses attention upon how decisions about dealing with young offenders are taken. A principal contention of the approach is that administrative decisions have become increasingly important in juvenile justice. Thus, the corporatist approach pinpoints the development of inter-agency collaboration, introduced to expedite decision-taking. One predicted consequence of these changes is increased official intervention in young people's lives to ensure behavioural containment.

These introductory comments only highlight some features of the corporatist approach and the conclusions drawn from our case study evidence are tentative. As argued in Chapter 8, the approach is most applicable to aspects of the management of young offenders at North City and Speke. Thus, Speke and North City participated in and/or organised inter-agency panels whose objectives were, variously, to decide what recommendations should be made to the police on cautioning and to the courts on sentencing. The overall objectives of the panels were to divert young people from the courts and from custody.

Inter-agency collaboration depends on different parties, who may not share similar values, agreeing common objectives. To use as an example the North City juvenile and cautioning panels, different professional perspectives were clearly evident in their discussions. In the first place, not all the district social workers on the juvenile panel declared themselves wholly committed to the 'tariff' system which the panel was instituted to help implement. But an even clearer indication of potentially conflicting positions was revealed in the comment of a cautioning panel member, that the cautioning panel would gain credibility if it were occasionally to recommend prosecution; an outcome quite contrary to the panel's aims. Despite the potential for disagreement, members of both panels argued that the panel process offered them an opportunity to air differing opinions and to reach decisions which, in some way, accommodated these differences.

What implications, in particular, did the cautioning panel system have for the young people concerned? One consequence was that personnel from different agencies could pool their knowledge about young people and their families. The researcher had no means of establishing whether there was any misuse of confidential information obtained in this way but the possibility was a source of concern to the Project leader in North City.

There was no apparent evidence in the operation of the North City cautioning panel to support the possibility – raised in the study of the Northampton Bureau (Davis, Boucherat and Watson, 1989) – that the system led to the needs of young people and their families being neglected. Although young people and their families did not attend cautioning panel meetings, the decisions of the panels were discussed with them and follow-up visits were arranged to a number of families to monitor and offer advice on issues of concern to the panel – such as suspected drug abuse.

The discussion of the cautioning panel here has focused on the work of a multi-agency panel which was efficiently run. What is less clear is what safeguards exist to ensure comparable standards of practice in all such panels. These forums take important decisions affecting the lives of young people, yet the deliberations are not open to those they most affect, nor to outside assessors.

In conclusion, the purpose of referring to the 'corporatist' approach here is to begin to draw attention to key features of the decision-making processes for dealing with young offenders. The panel system clearly differs from formal court proceedings. The trauma and delays experienced by young people appearing in court and the variations in sentencing outcomes have justifiably been widely criticised. Less information is yet available about the impact of newer administrative arrangements for dealing with young offenders at the lower end of the tariff.

Conclusion

The conclusion of the case studies was that project staff strove to serve young people's interests by increasing the range of pre-court and pre-custody options. How widespread, 'just' or uniform such procedures are seems an important topic for further research.

The role of the voluntary agency

The researcher discussed Barnardo's involvement in providing intermediate treatment services with social services management and fieldwork staff in the three districts where the case study projects were located. It should be remembered, though, that the views obtained were not from a complete cross-section of staff but rather from those with close links with the projects. Thus, the social work managers had nearly all been closely involved in liaising with Barnardo's in planning and establishing the projects. And the objectives of individual projects, whether solely justice-oriented or more broadly framed, still reflected the commitments and philosophies of these managers. The field social workers with whom the care-related work of Boughton Hall and Speke was discussed were those who had made recent referrals to these programmes. It might be judged, then, that these staff had some evidence of, and trust in, the quality of the projects' work. Referrals to the alternative-to-custody programmes were, however, ultimately made by the courts and, in contrast, the social workers interviewed because they were allocated to act as supervising officers for *these* cases did not, necessarily, have a prior commitment to the projects.

   Most respondents recognised that collaboration between the statutory and voluntary sectors is one face of the mixed economy of welfare fostered, as discussed in Chapter 1, by the policies of the Conservative Government which had been in power for over a decade. An enhanced role for the voluntary sector and increased reliance on its resources were accepted facts of welfare life. There were, nevertheless, clear divisions in the views of social services staff.

   Some respondents welcomed the links that had been forged between Barnardo's and their local authority. Their collective perception was of a voluntary sector, comparatively unfettered by statutory and bureaucratic requirements, which was allowed to be innovative in its work. Their more detailed assessments were, however, based on the perceived efficiency of local Barnardo's staff, and confidence that their objectives and styles of working were in accord with those of the local authority concerned. With one or two exceptions, Barnardo's staff and the achievements of the projects were highly praised.

   The alternative perspective – more critical of Barnardo's role – stemmed, in part, from disapproval of Government policies which encouraged more dependence on the contribution of the voluntary sector. In Liverpool, the quality of service which Barnardo's could finance – at a time of local authority cutbacks and major local controversies and difficulties – was contrasted with what was certainly perceived as less well-resourced local authority provision. It was argued that local authorities have to provide universal services for those who require them and meet the relevant criteria, whereas Barnardo's provides a geographically selective service. The fear was that voluntary sector involvement had led to inequities in service provision across the city.

Some respondents, while expressing a clear preference for well-funded state welfare, nevertheless valued the work actually undertaken in their area by Barnardo's staff. Others had further reservations. They doubted how appropriate it was that, what was termed 'statutory' work should be undertaken by a 'voluntary' body. For example, some respondents queried whether in difficult and sensitive areas of practice, such as cases of suspected abuse, Barnardo's staff had to meet the same guidelines of practice to which local authority social workers were subject.

Barnardo's will continue to endeavour to further its childcare aims by developing and expanding its work as seems appropriate. The preferences of local authority staff for well-funded state provision can hardly be addressed by the charity. What Barnardo's *is* able to influence is the quality of collaboration between the statutory and voluntary sectors. We think that the research study has assisted this process. One suggestion emanating from the case studies is the possibility of setting up local channels of communication, to ensure that local authority fieldwork staff, often responsible for collaboration over individual cases, are well-informed about the objectives and standards of practice operated by Barnardo's North-West Division. Local authority practitioners might also be offered opportunities to comment on their experiences to Divisional as well as local, Barnardo's staff.

Finally, it is worth highlighting Barnardo's refreshing commitment to subjecting its practice to scrutiny. Furthermore, the agency is committed to applying research findings where this is appropriate. The final section of the report will discuss how the research findings reported in this book were shared with the local authorities in discussions about renewing partnership agreements.

172   CONCLUSIONS

Utilising the research

The utilisation of research findings is a complex issue which has attracted considerable debate. At a macro-level, the prognosis has often been somewhat gloomy. Thus one analyst summarised the relationship between social research and policy in the following terms

'...despite the expenditure of some £50m a year on social research, in the 1980s the relationship between social research and government policy is exceedingly tenuous...To organise research as a problem-solving instrument – even within government departments – is...to court disappointment.' (Thomas in Loney, Boswell and Clarke (eds), 1983, p.117)

When social research has apparently influenced policy – Bowlby's maternal deprivation thesis is a much-quoted example – it has been said to be because the research was timely and accorded with the views of policy-makers.

A strategy suggested by Cherns (Cherns, 1979) to encourage wider application of research results was for findings to be fed into the policy making process where policy was permeable. A hopeful point of entry for the introduction of new information is at the stage of re-evaluation, following the appearance of discrepancies between aims and achievement. Barnardo's practice of subjecting its practice in the childcare field to regular re-evaluation is, in a sense, a variant of this strategy and one which offers the promise of fruitful use of research materials.

How then have the results of the case studies reported here been disseminated? And is there any evidence of their being utilised? As far as the dissemination of findings is concerned, once each case study was complete, working documents reporting the findings were made available to Project staff for consideration. Comments made by staff at this stage enabled the researcher to amend inaccuracies and ambiguities and, importantly, offered a framework for project discussions about current practice and procedures.

The working papers were next circulated by Barnardo's to the relevant local authority managers. These papers provided the initial agenda for a series of discussions, between the responsible Assistant Director in Barnardo's and the local authority social services managers in each of the districts where the research was undertaken. The case study reports provided up to date information which the managers could use in determining:

- whether it was mutually acceptable for each project to continue working as it had been;
- whether there would be benefits to be gained by setting new or revised objectives for individual projects, in order to adapt to new demands or to build on existing strengths;
- whether there was a case for radically reviewing the future development of a project.

Following this review process some changes were proposed in the organisation and objectives of the case study centres. The research study, arguably, was one of several significant factors influencing change.

In Liverpool, plans to implement a full re-organisation of all social services in 1991 are unlikely to go ahead, because of the severe financial problems faced by the City. As far as the intermediate treatment centres in the study are concerned, following their review it was agreed that the objectives of the North City Centre should remain unchanged. The Project will continue to work solely and specifically with known offenders.

In contrast, the objectives of the Speke centre have been revised. From 1 April 1991 the centre became known as the South City Young People's Resource Centre. Its aims, in descending order of importance, are:

- the primary function of the Centre will be to provide community-based alternatives to admissions to care for children and young people aged 10-17 years;
- the secondary function of the centre is to facilitate the early discharge of children and young people already in care through the provision of community-based support packages;
- the third function of the centre is to provide community-based alternatives for children and young people at risk of custody. This will include co-ordination of the Juvenile Liaison Scheme (Cautioning Scheme). (Revised aims and objectives agreed November 1990.)

These objectives virtually reverse those previously set. Greatest emphasis is placed upon the alternative-to-care work and least on the alternative-to-custody work. These priorities do, though, apparently reflect the relative strengths of the centre recorded during the research study.

In Chester District, the review meetings focused even more specifically upon the initial research document. Local authority and Barnardo's staff were in agreement over one of the main issues raised during the research, that the criteria for accepting referrals to the care-related programmes needed to be more carefully specified. At the time of writing, the possibility of segregating alternative-to-care and alternative-to-custody work is also under consideration. With the merger of the Ellesmere Port and Chester Districts, it would be possible for Boughton Hall to specialise in care-related work and for the Ellesmere Port team to undertake the alternative-to-custody work.

Ostensibly, then, the research findings have made a significant contribution. They appear, variously:

- to have framed the terms of the review meetings;
- to have focused attention upon the strengths of individual projects which should be maintained or developed – clear examples are the justice work at North City and the care-related work with girls at Speke;
- to have pinpointed more contentious and challenging problems – examples are the mixing of young offenders with young people with care-related needs at the more broadly-based projects, and the need to agree stricter criteria for entry onto care-related programmes at Boughton Hall.

It would, however, be simplistic to ignore some other factors which will have influenced the content and outcome of the reviews of the three projects.

First of all, it is worth stressing that such a review process would not have taken place were it not for Barnardo's willingness to expose its procedures and practice to research investigation and, subsequently, to establish mechanisms for implementing such changes as seemed desirable.

A second factor affecting the outcomes of the review process was the re-structuring exercises, which both Liverpool and Chester were undergoing at the time the research studies were being undertaken.

Finally, and particularly influential, is the changing legislative context. Two issues are particularly pertinent for those planning services for young people. One is the emphasis in the Children Act 1989 on the responsibility of local authorities to discourage offending behaviour. The relative roles of intermediate treatment and other

youth provisions in fulfilling this responsibility remains to be seen –
nevertheless, the Act would appear to endorse the continuance of
projects specialising in 'preventive' work.

The other issue is the Government's intention to raise the age limit
for the juvenile – or youth – court to 18 years. This proposal was
mooted in the Green Paper, *Punishment, Custody and the Community*
(1988), because of the more severe treatment of young adult
offenders as compared with juveniles, despite essential similarities in
offending behaviour. And, following modifications in the subsequent White Paper (1990), in November 1990 the proposal was
included in the new Criminal Justice Bill. If the proposals become
law, the evidence of the case studies suggests that this new area of
work would pose significant challenges. Juvenile justice centres
would have to be prepared for an influx of young adults and for
working increasingly with those who are already heavily involved in
criminal activities. Furthermore, these young adults would almost
certainly have already completed a range of community-based
sentencing options, so project staff would have to develop new
programmes appropriate for them. We would suggest that centres
which specialise in justice work are better placed to be able to cope
with the anticipated new demands than more broadly-based centres.

Overall, it is encouraging that the research programme described
in this book seems to have made a contribution to the development of
services for vulnerable young people in the North-West. It is seldom
that researchers are offered such an opportunity and we are indebted
to the far-sightedness of Barnardo's for enabling this to happen.

References

Ames, J., *Hard Bargains, A Study of Inter-Agency Collaboration in the Provision of Day Care*. Unpublished M.Phil thesis: Open University: 1986.

Atkinson, D., *Boughton Hall Intermediate Treatment Project Reports*. Barnardo's: mimeo: 1989, 1989 and 1985.

Ball, C., 'Major Crimes: A Need for Custodial Regimes?' in Doyle S. (ed.), *Towards a Custody Free Community*. Association of Juvenile Justice: n.d.

Ball, C., 'Secret Justice: The Use Made of School Reports in the Juvenile Court', in *British Journal of Social Work*, Volume 13: 1983.

Blagg, H., 'Reparation and Justice for Juveniles: The Corby Experience', in *British Journal of Criminology*, Volume 25, no. 7: 1985.

Bottoms, A., 'Cambridge Research into Intermediate Treatment' in *Youth Social Work*, no 5: 1987.

Bottoms, A., and others, *Intermediate Treatment and Juvenile Justice: Key Findings and Implications from a National Survey of Intermediate Treatment Policy and Practice*. London: HMSO: 1990.

Box, S., *Deviance, Reality and Society*. London: Holt, Rinehart and Winston: 1971.

Bryman, A., (ed.), *Doing Research in Organisations*. London: Routledge: 1988.

Cherns, A., *Using the Social Sciences*. London: Routledge: 1979.

Cheshire County Council, *Cheshire Current Facts and Figures, Population and Vital Statistics*: Pop A12. Cheshire: 1988.

Cheshire County Council, *Unemployment Rates by Ward*. Research and Intelligence Section: Cheshire: 1989

Cheshire County Council, *Areas of Family Stress Reports*. Research and Intelligence Section: Cheshire: 1983 and 1985.

Cheshire Social Services Committee, *Report of the Director of Social Services, Director of Education, Chief Probation Officer and Chief Constable*: Review of Juvenile Justice Policy: Cheshire: mimeo: 1987.

Clarke, R., 'Jack Tizard Memorial Lecture: Delinquency, Environment and Intervention', in *Journal of Child Pyschology and Psychiatry*, Volume 26, No. 4: 1985.

Cohen, S., *Folk Devils and Moral Panics*. St Albans: Paladin: 1972.

Colenso, D., *Speke Intermediate Treatment Project Reports*. Barnardo's: mimeo: 1988.

Copp, A. Mummery, S. and Rae, H., *Liverpool Juvenile Justice Monitoring System Statistics*, Liverpool Social Services Department: 1987.

Copp, A. Mummery, S. and Rae, H., *Liverpool Juvenile Justice Monitoring System Statistics*. Liverpool Social Services Department: 1988.

Craig, N., *Liverpool North City Intermediate Treatment Project* Barnardo's: mimeo: 1985.

Curtis, S., *Juvenile Offending, Prevention Through Intermediate Treatment*. London: Batsford: 1989.

Davis, G., Boucherat, J., and Watson, D., 'Pre-court Decision Making in Juvenile Justice', in *British Journal of Criminology*, Volume 29, No. 3: 1989.

De'Ath, E., 'The Challenge of Diversion', in *Youth in Society*, August 1988.

Denman, G., *Intensive Intermediate Treatment with Juvenile Offenders: A Handbook on Assessment and Groupwork Practice*. University of Lancaster: Centre of Youth, Crime and Community: n.d.

DHSS, *Intermediate Treatment (LAC(77)1)*. London: DHSS: 1977.

DHSS, *Further Development of Intermediate Treatment*. Circular LAC(83)3): London: DHSS: 1983.

DHSS, *Reports to Courts: Practice Guidance for Social Workers*. London: HMSO: 1987.

Dixon, N., *An Exploratory Study of the Speke, North City and Boughton Hall Intermediate Treatment Centres*. Barnardo's: mimeo: 1988.

DoH, *Children in the Care of the Local Authorities*. Personal Social Services: Local Authority Statistics: 1987.

Downie, J., and Ames, J., *Intermediate Treatment Research*. Social Services Monographs: University of Sheffield: 1981.

Farrington, D., 'Delinquency Prevention in the 1980s', in *Journal of Adolescence*, Volume 8: 1985.

Farrington, D., 'Implications of Criminal Career Research for the Prevention of Offending', in *Journal of Adolescence*, Volume 13: 1990.

Harris, R., 'Towards Just Welfare: A Consideration of Current Contraversy in the Theory of Juvenile Justice', in *British Journal of Criminology*, Volume 25, No. 1: 1985.

Hoghughi, M., *The Delinquent: Directions for Social Control*, London: Hutchinson: 1983.

Holman, R., *Kids at the Door*. Oxford: Blackwell: 1981.

Home Office, *Children in Trouble*. Cmnd 3601: HMSO: 1968.

Home Office, *Social Inquiry Reports; General Guidance on Contents to Sentencing*. (Circular 17/83): London: Home Office: 1983.

Home Office, *The Cautioning of Offenders*. (Circular 14/85): London: HMSO: 1985.

Home Office, *Social Inquiry Reports*, (Circular 92/86): London: HMSO: 1986.

Home Office, *Punishment, Custody and the Community*. Cmnd 424: HMSO: 1988.

180

REFERENCES

Home Office, *Criminal Statistics in England and Wales 1988*. HMSO: 1989.

Home Office, *Crime, Justice and Protecting the Public*. Cmnd/965: HMSO: 1990.

Jarrett, R. and Cormick, R., *Boughton Hall Intermediate Treatment Project*. Social Services Department: Chester District: mimeo: 1986.

Jones, R., 'Questioning the New Orthodoxy', in *Community Care*, October 11: 1984.

Knapp, M. and Robertson, E., 'The Costs of Services' in Kahan., B. (ed.), *Child Care Research, Policy and Practice*. London: Hodder & Stoughton: 1989.

Marris, P. and Rein, M., *Dilemmas of Social Reform*. Harmondsworth: Penguin: 1967.

Morris, A. and Giller, H., *Understanding Juvenile Justice*. London: Croom Helm: 1987.

NACRO, *Diverting Juveniles from Custody: Findings from the Fourth Census of Projects funded under the DHSS IT Initiative*. London: NACRO: 1987(a).

NACRO, *Race and Juvenile Justice*. London: NACRO: 1987(b).

NACRO, *Some Facts About Juvenile Crime*. London: NACRO: 1989a.

NACRO, *Progress Through Partnership*. London: NACRO: 1989b.

Parker, H. Sumner, M. and Jarvis, G., *Unmasking the Magistrates*. Milton Keynes: Open University Press: 1989.

Parsloe, P., 'Social Work and the Justice Model', in *British Journal of Social Work*, Volume 6, No. 1: 1976.

Pitts, J., *The Politics of Juvenile Crime*. London: Sage: 1988.

Pitts, J., *Working with Young Offenders*. Basingstoke: Macmillan: 1990.

Report of the Committee on Children and Young Persons 1960. (Chairman: Viscount Ingleby), Cmnd 1191, HMSO.

Pratt, J., 'Juvenile Justice, Social Work and Social Control. The Need for Positive Thinking', in *British Journal of Social Work*, Volume 15: 1985.

Pratt, J., 'Corporatism: The Third Model of Juvenile Justice', in *British Journal of Criminology*, Volume 29, No. 3: 1989.

Prison Reform Trust, *The Route from Care to Custody*. Juvenile Justice Project: Report No. 2: London: Prison Reform Trust: 1988.

Richardson, N., 'No end to juvenile custody?', in *Childright*, December 1989.

Rogowski, S., 'Radical Intermediate Treatment: Some Views from the Field', in *Youth and Policy*, No. 29, April: 1990.

Rutherford, A., *Growing Out of Crime: Society and Young People in Trouble*. Harmondsworth: Penguin: 1986.

Rutter, M. and Giller, R., *Juvenile Delinquency: Trends and Perspectives*. Harmondsworth: Penguin: 1983.

Ryan, W., *The Social Welfare Client: Blaming the Victim*. Orback & Chambers: 1971.

Social Information Systems Ltd, *Juvenile Justice in Cheshire 1984-1986. A Review*. Cheshire County Council: n.d.

Stafford, E., and Hill, J., 'The Tariff, Social Enquiry Reports and the Sentencing of Juveniles', in *British Journal of Criminology*. Volume 27, No. 4: 1987.

Thomas, P., 'Social Research and Government Policy', in Loney, M., Boswell, D. and Clarke, J. (eds), *Social Policy and Social Welfare*. Milton Keynes: Open University; 1983.

Thorpe, D., and others, *Out of Care: The Community Support of Juvenile Offenders*. London: Allen and Unwin: 1980.

Warner, N., 'Out of the Blue', in *Social Services Insight*, No. 2, Volume 40: 1989.

West, D., and Farrington, D. *Who Becomes Delinquent?* London: Heinemann: 1973.

Young, J., *The Drugtakers*. London: Paladin: 1971.

Index